80'S ROCKERS

&

STRESS RELIEVING HIPPIE ROCKERS

ROCK COLORING BOOK

2 BOOK BUNDLE

80's ROCKERS

Rock Coloring Book

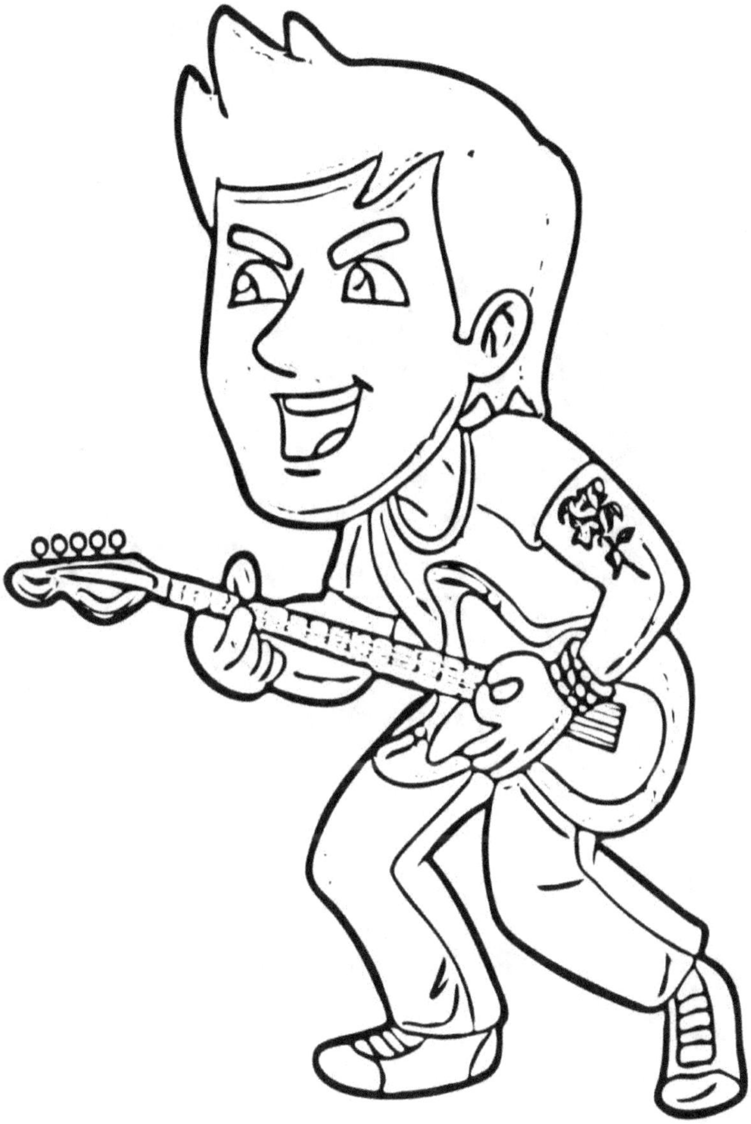

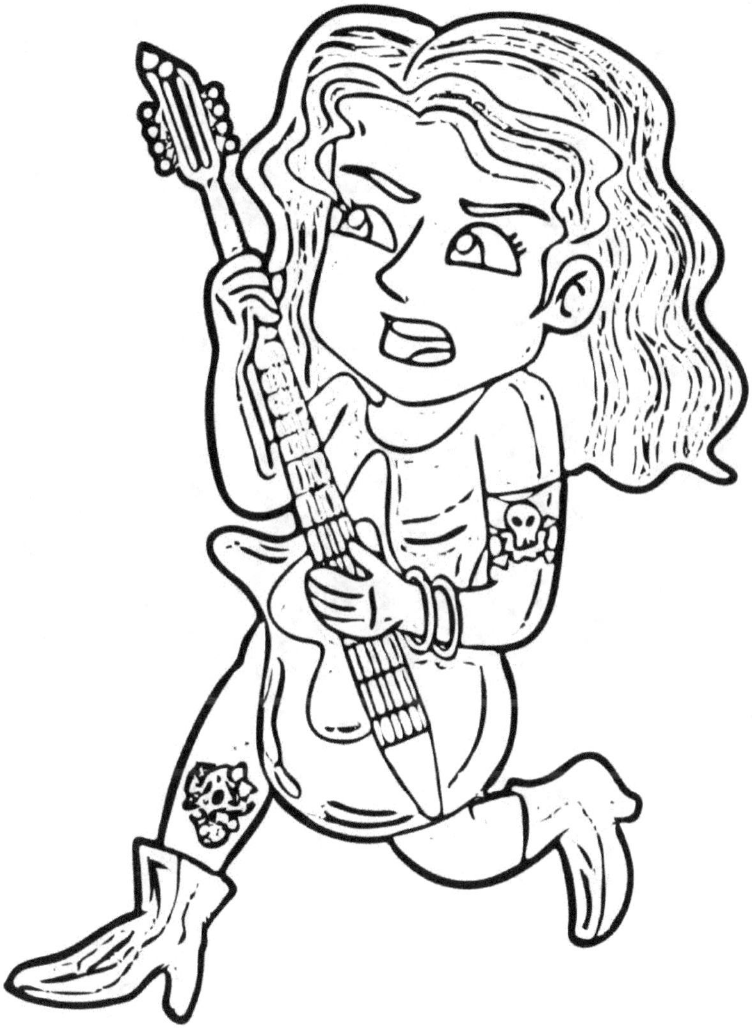

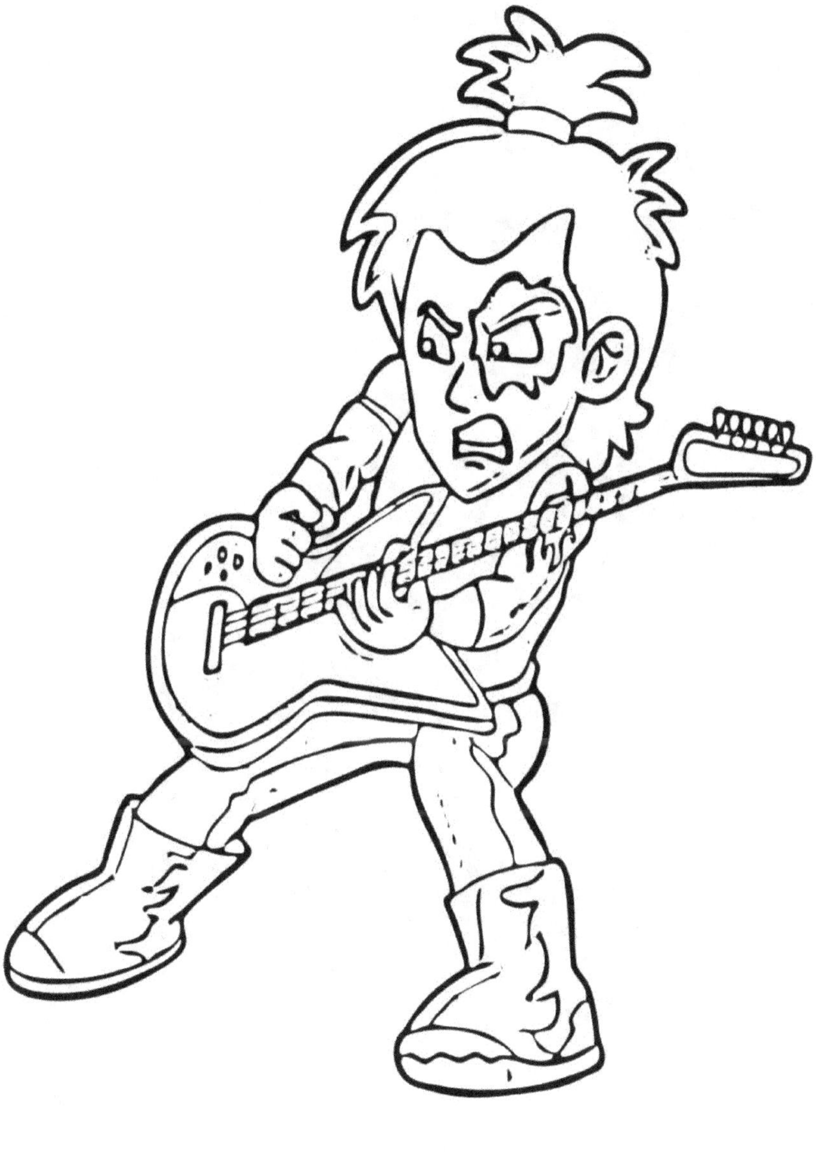

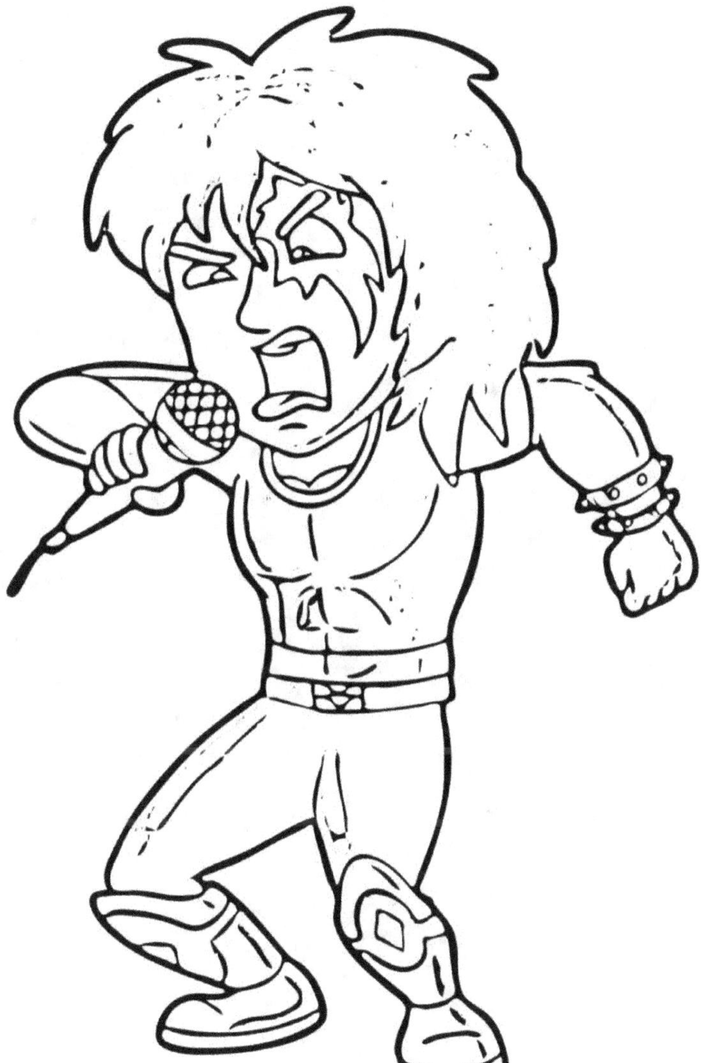

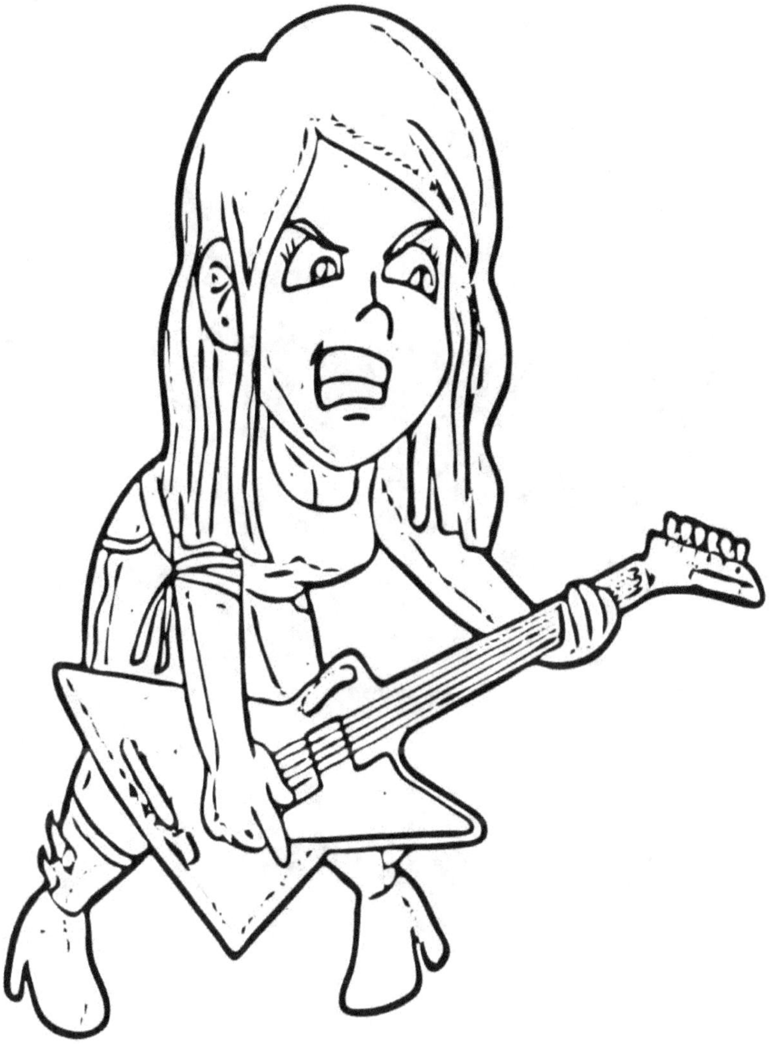

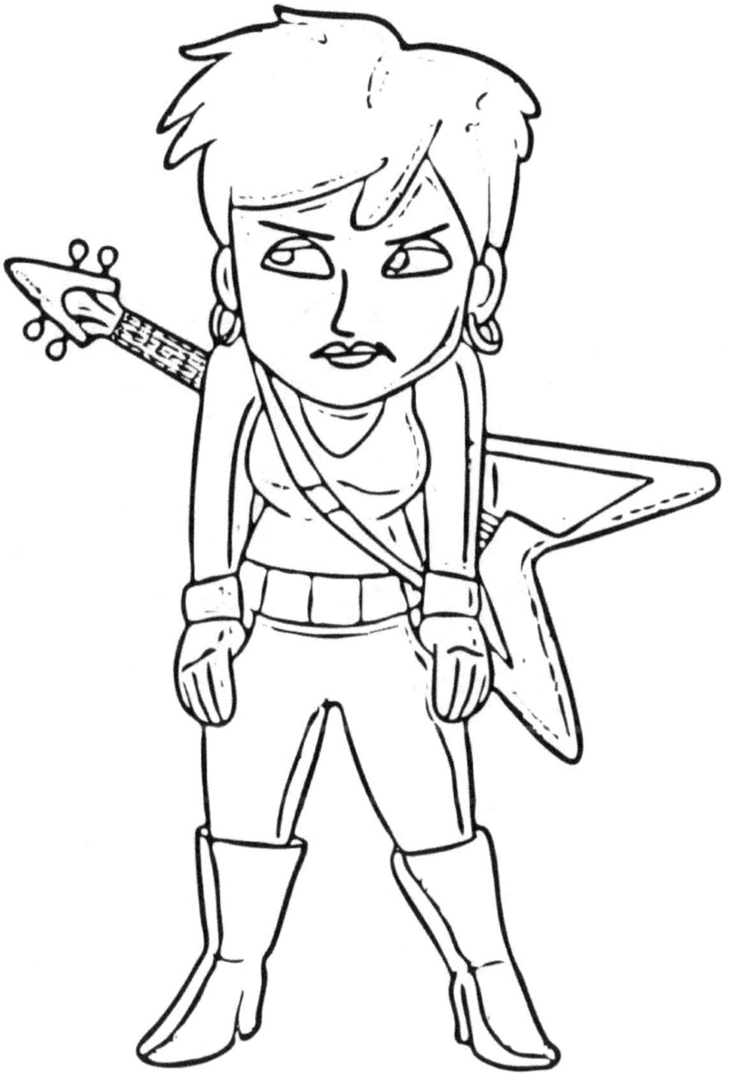

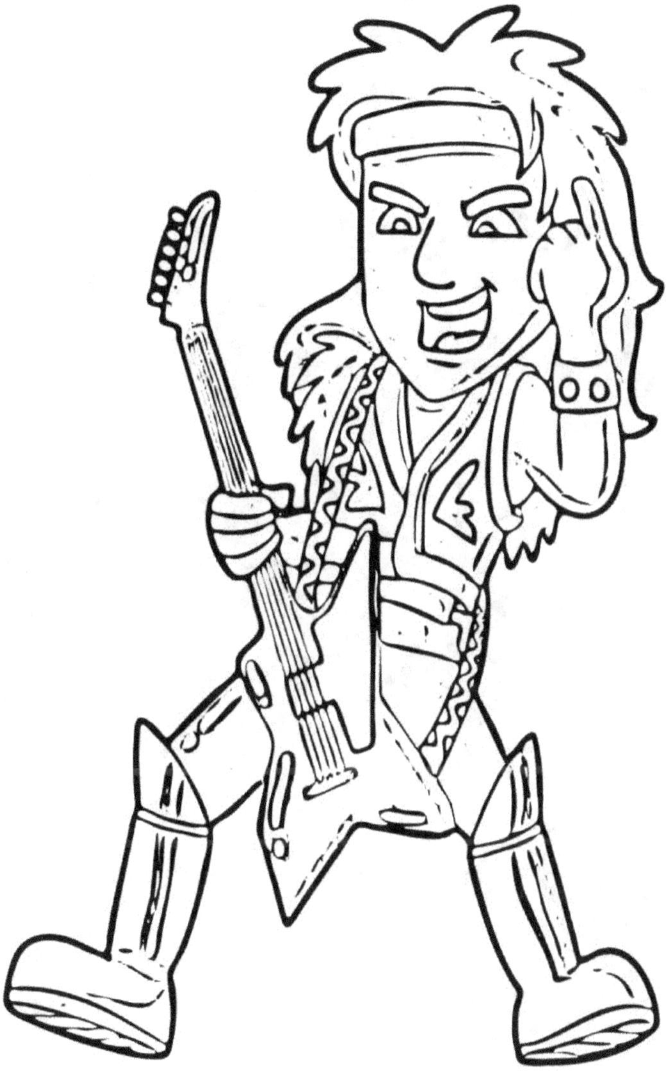

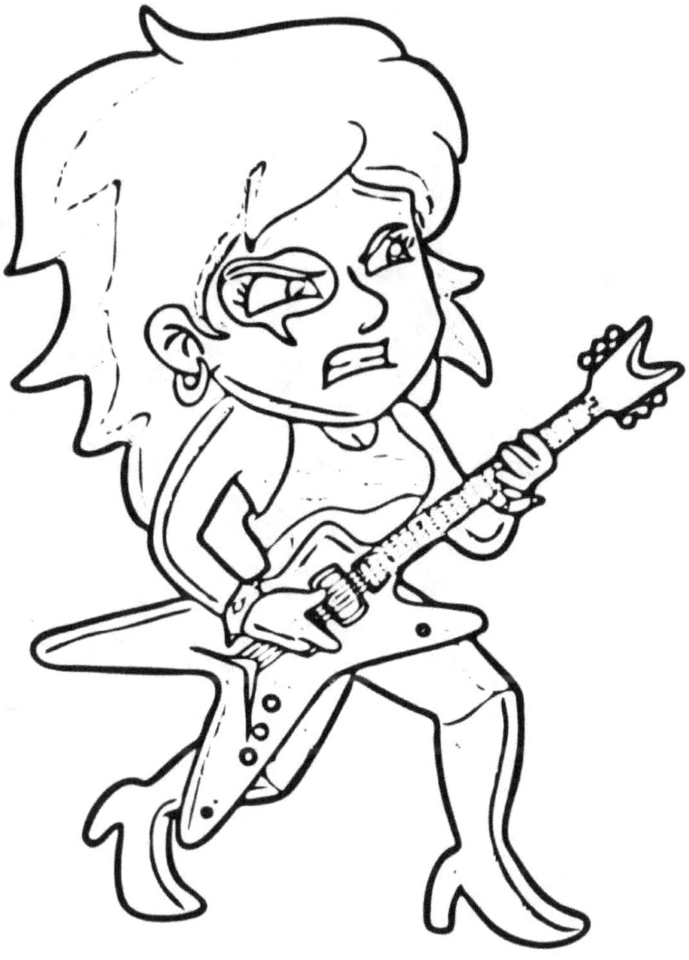

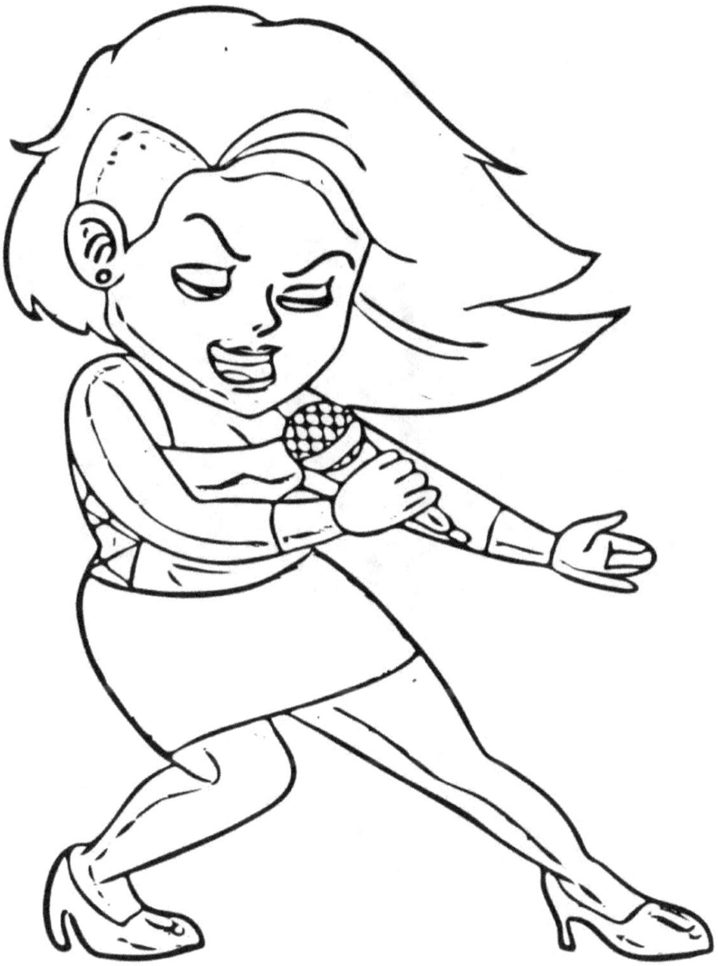

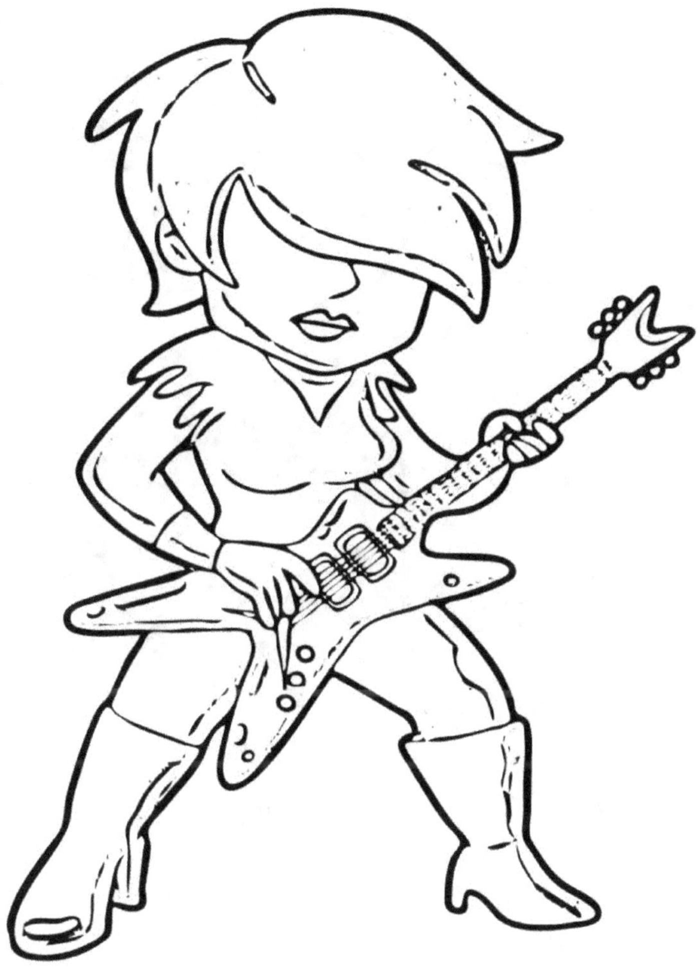

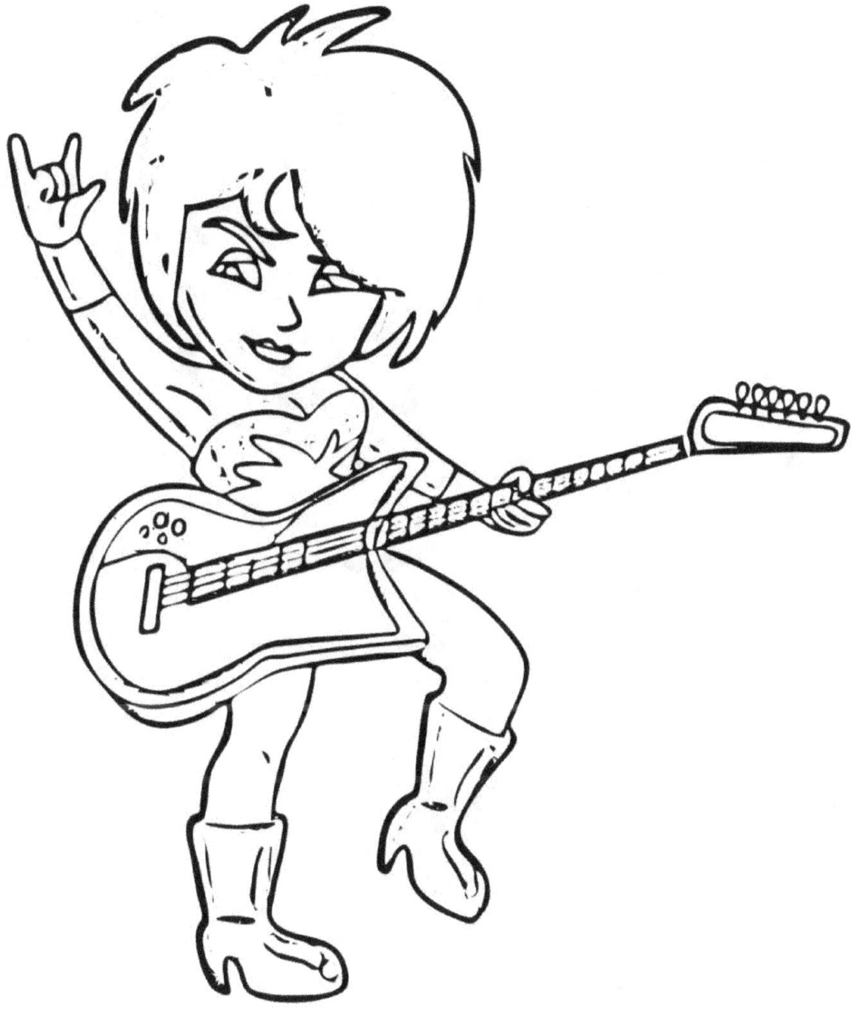

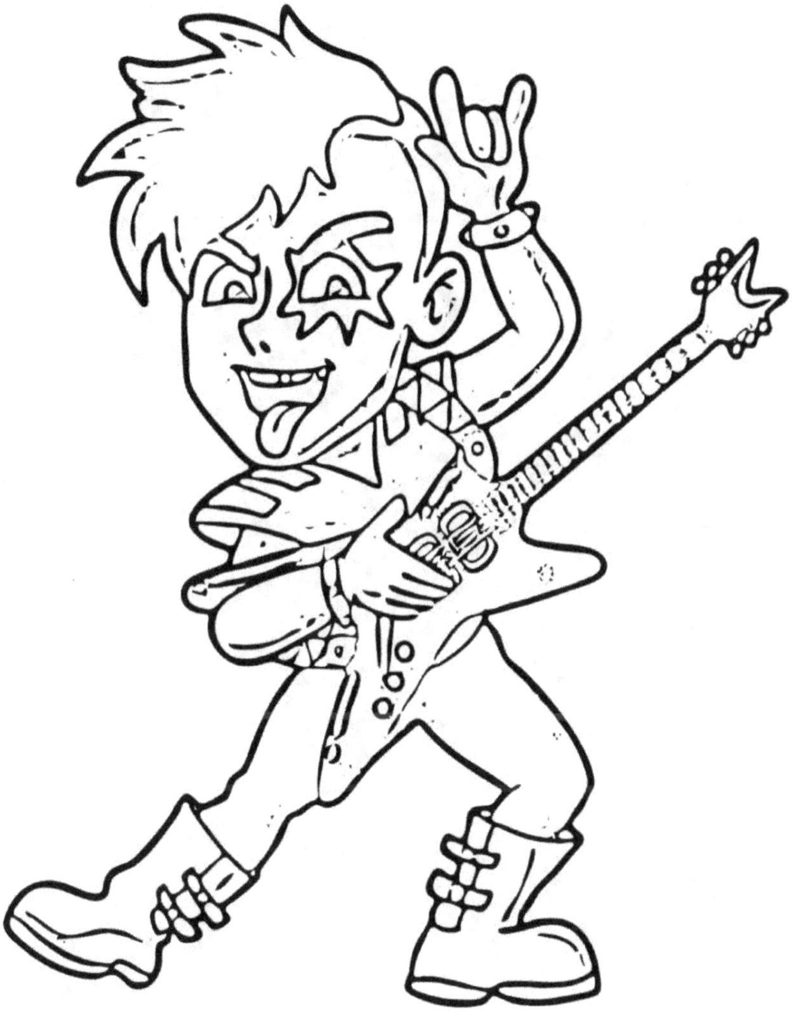

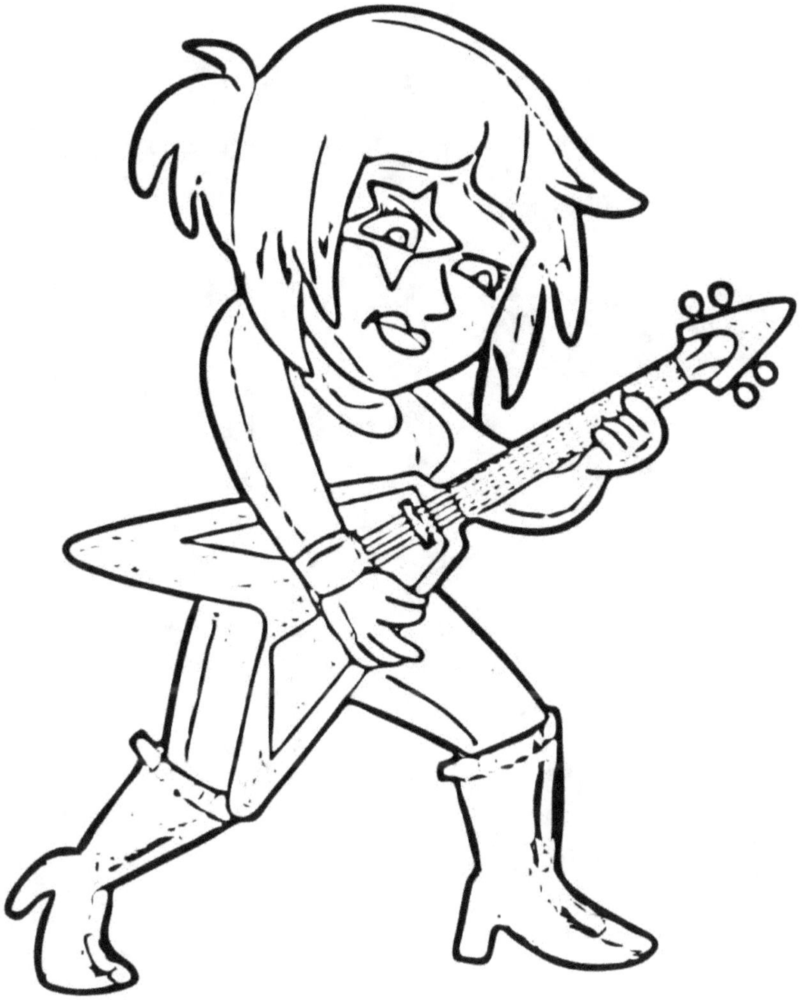

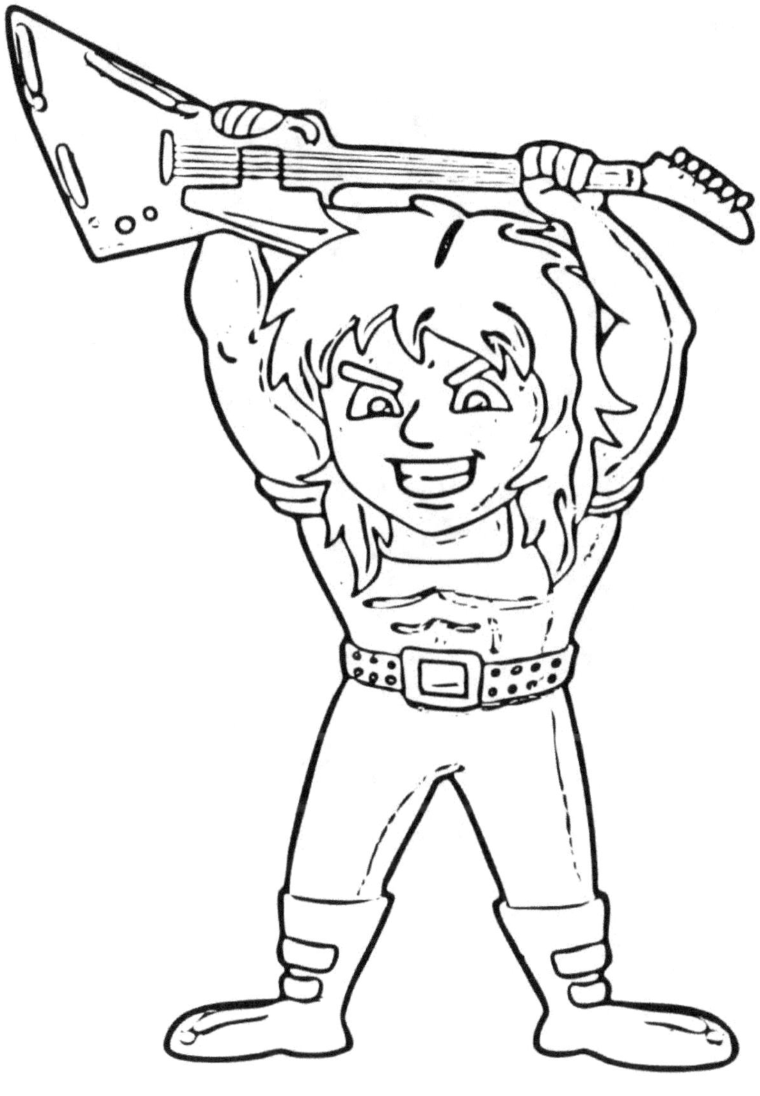

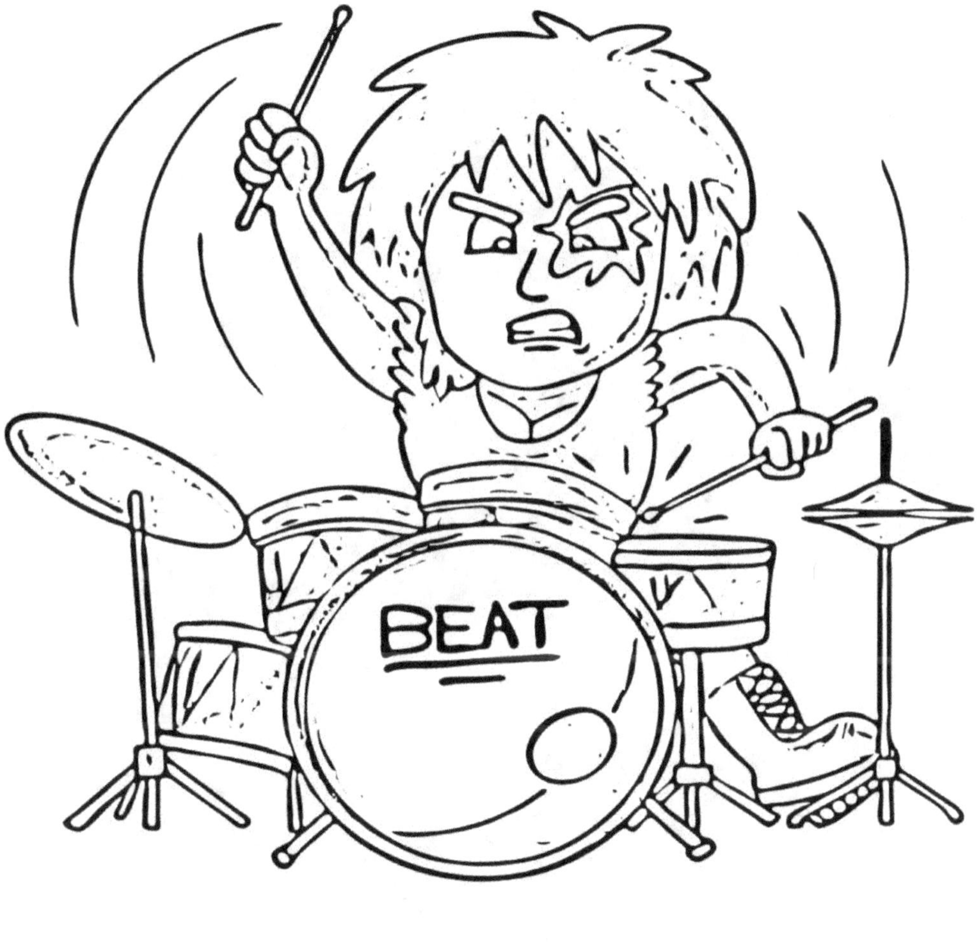
BEAT

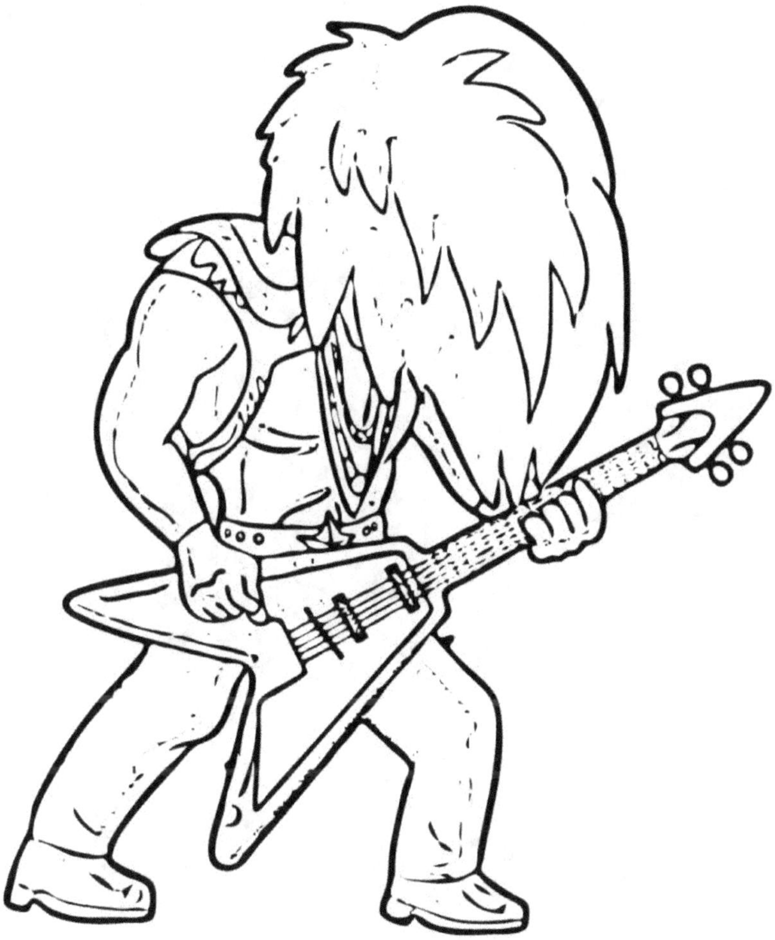

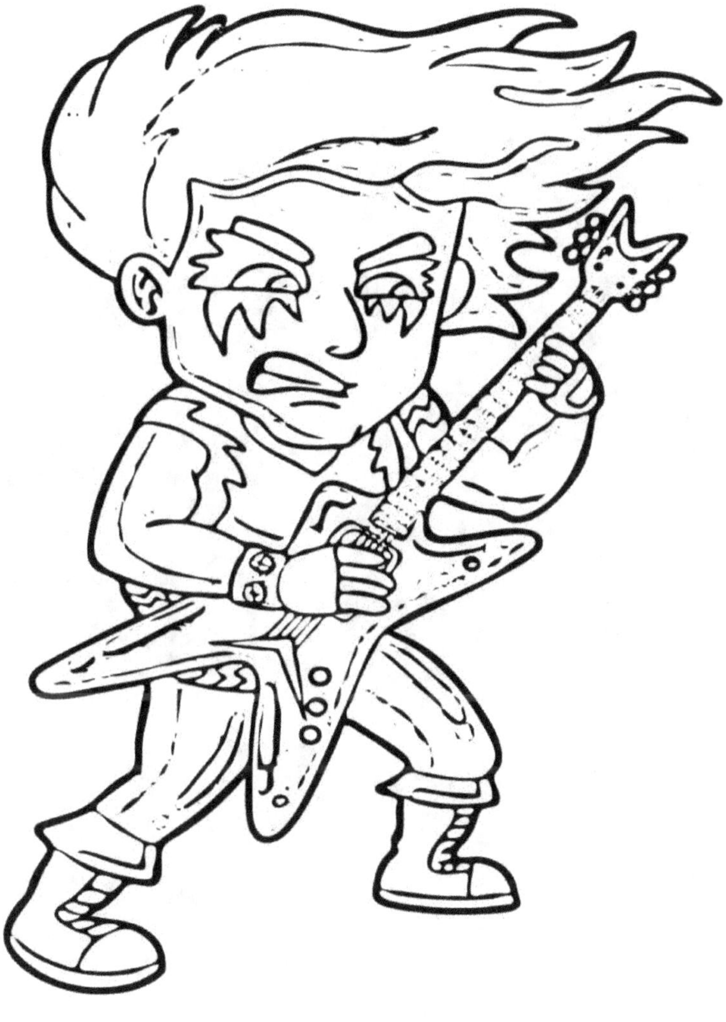

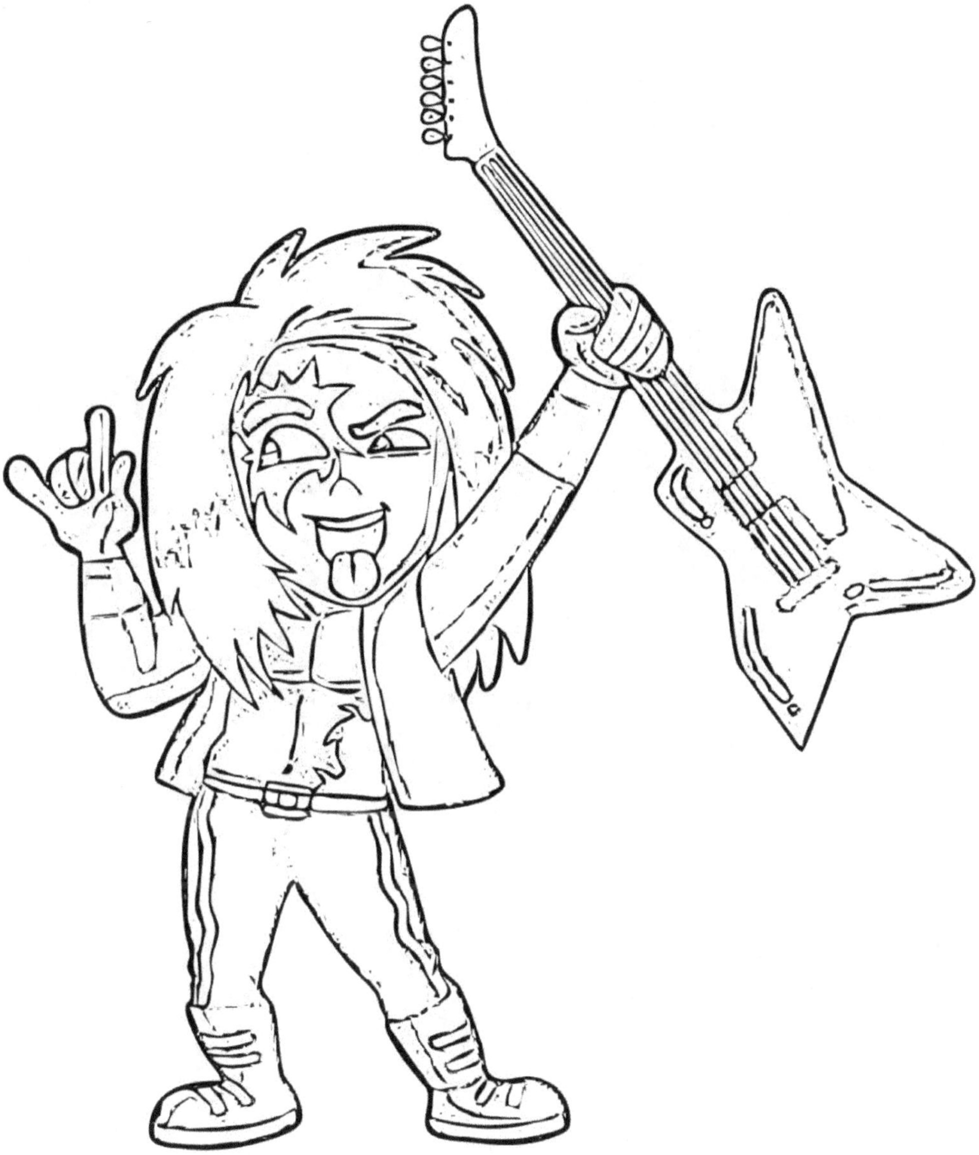

Stress Relieving HIPPIE ROCKERS

Rock Coloring Book

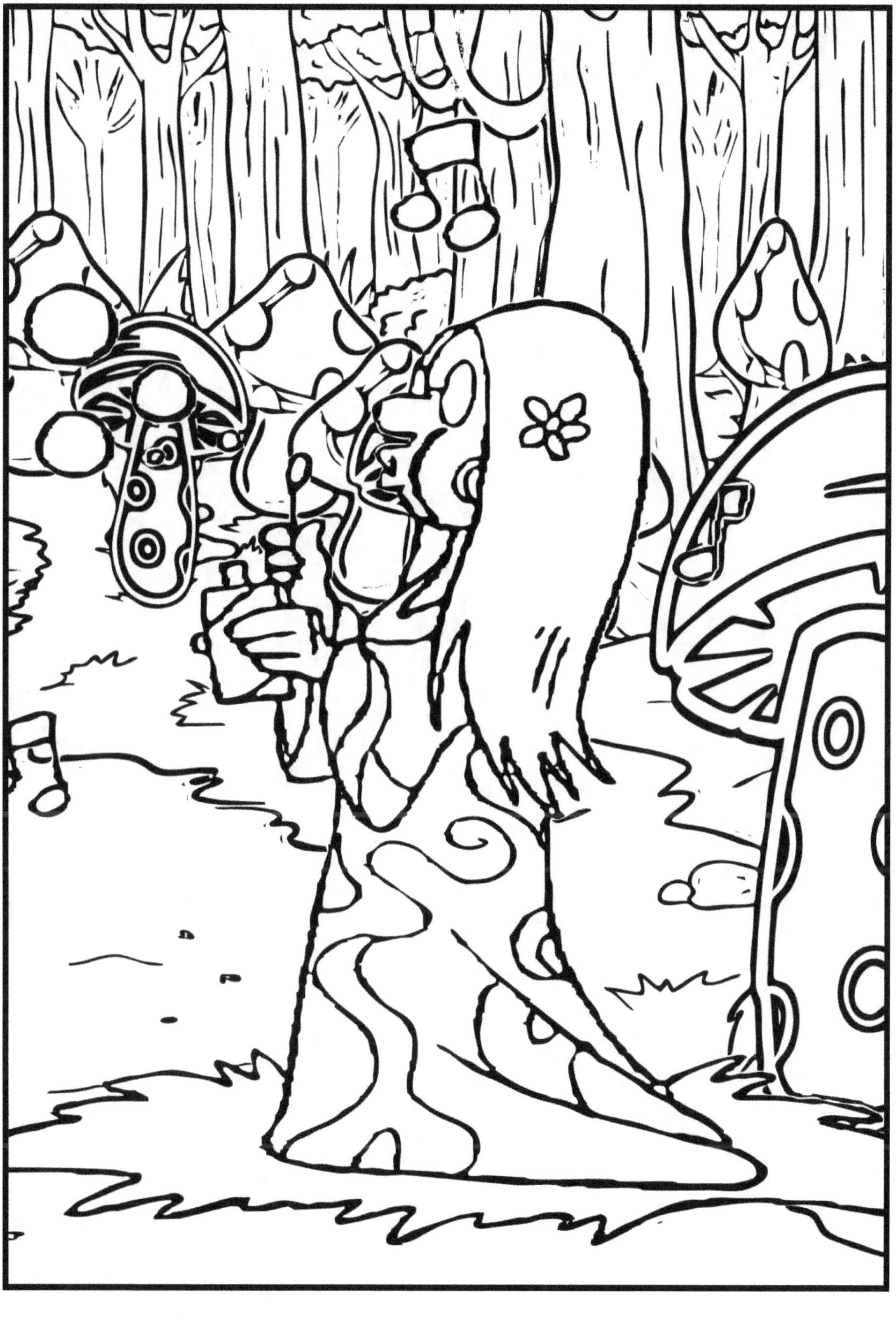

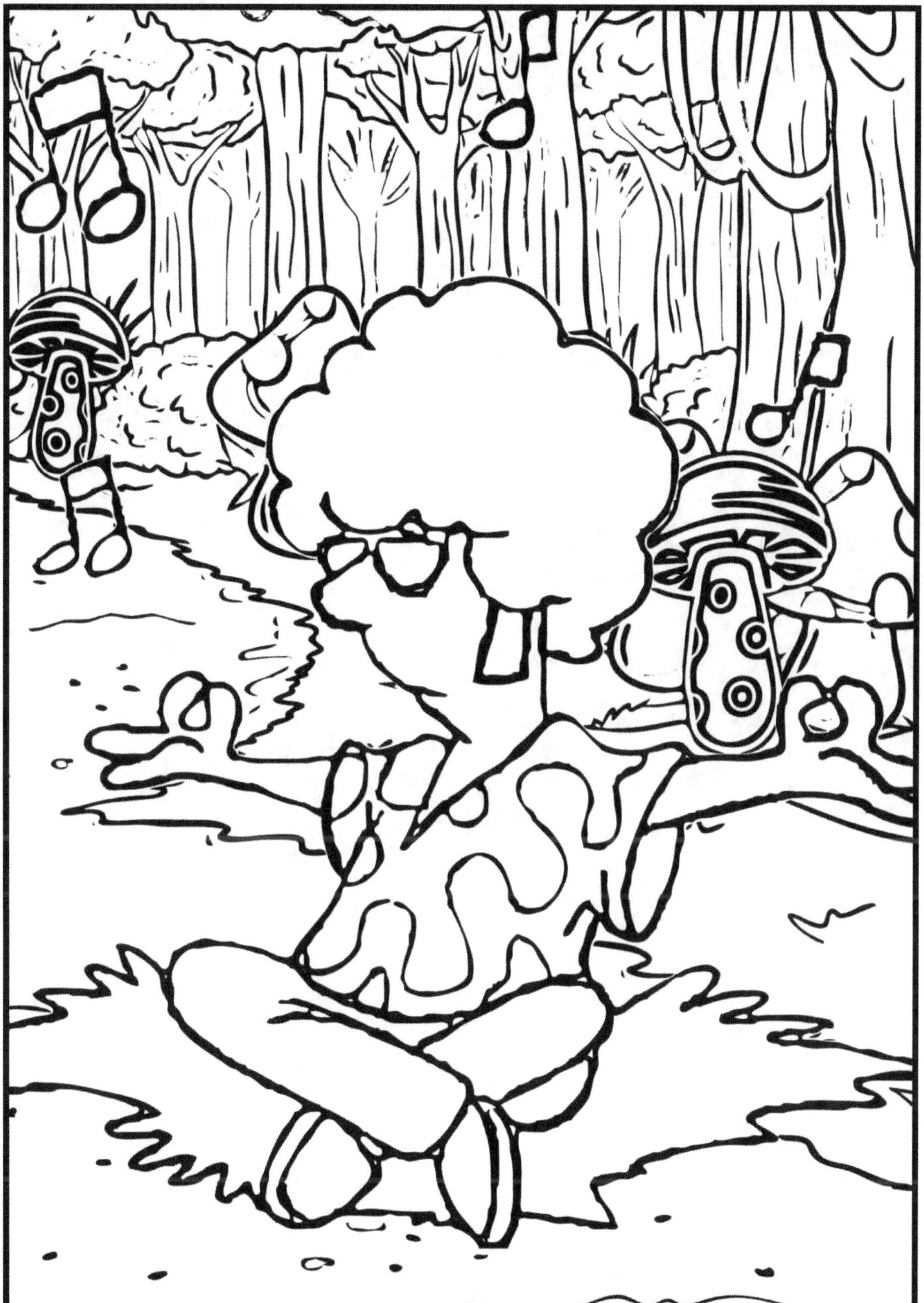

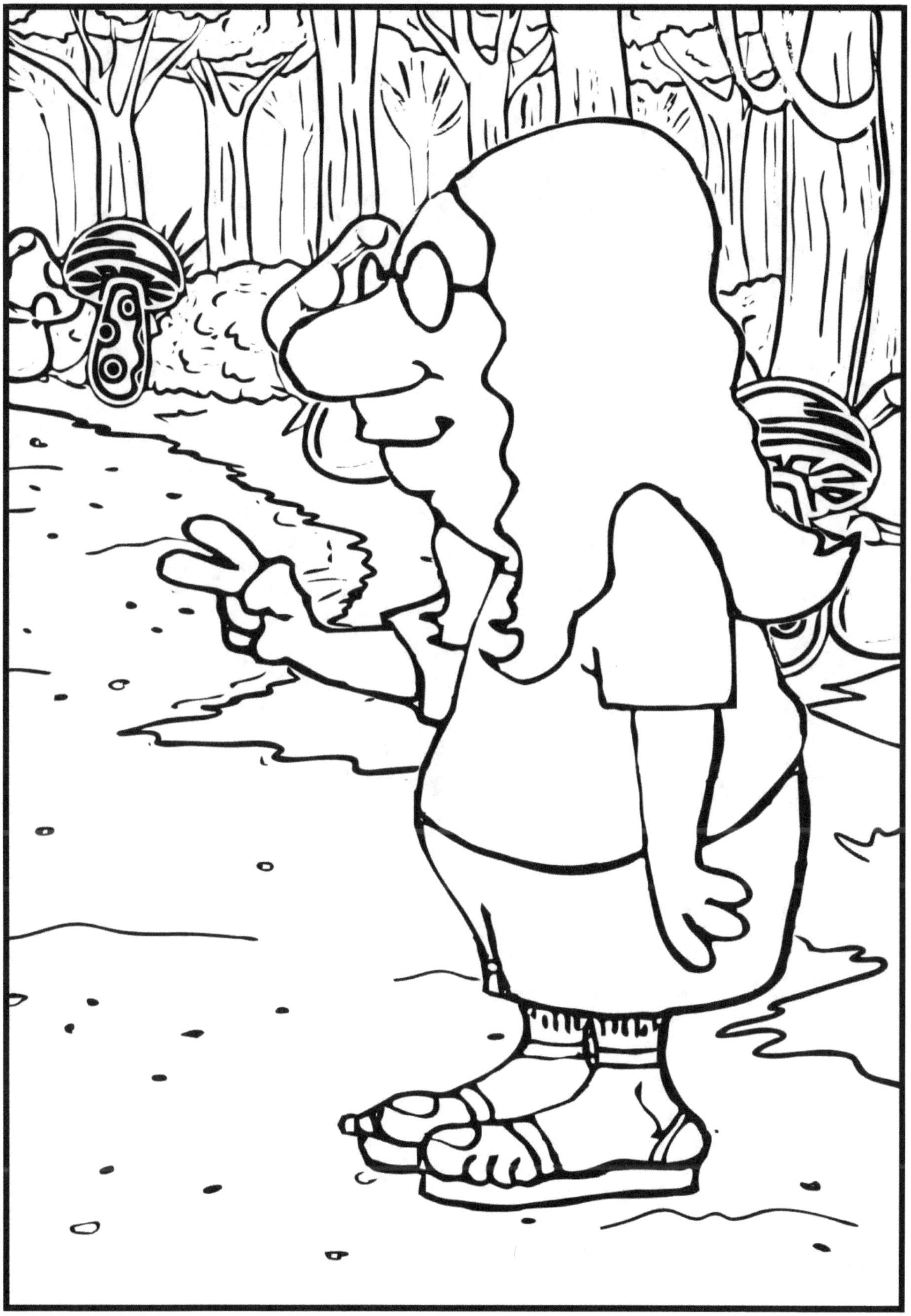

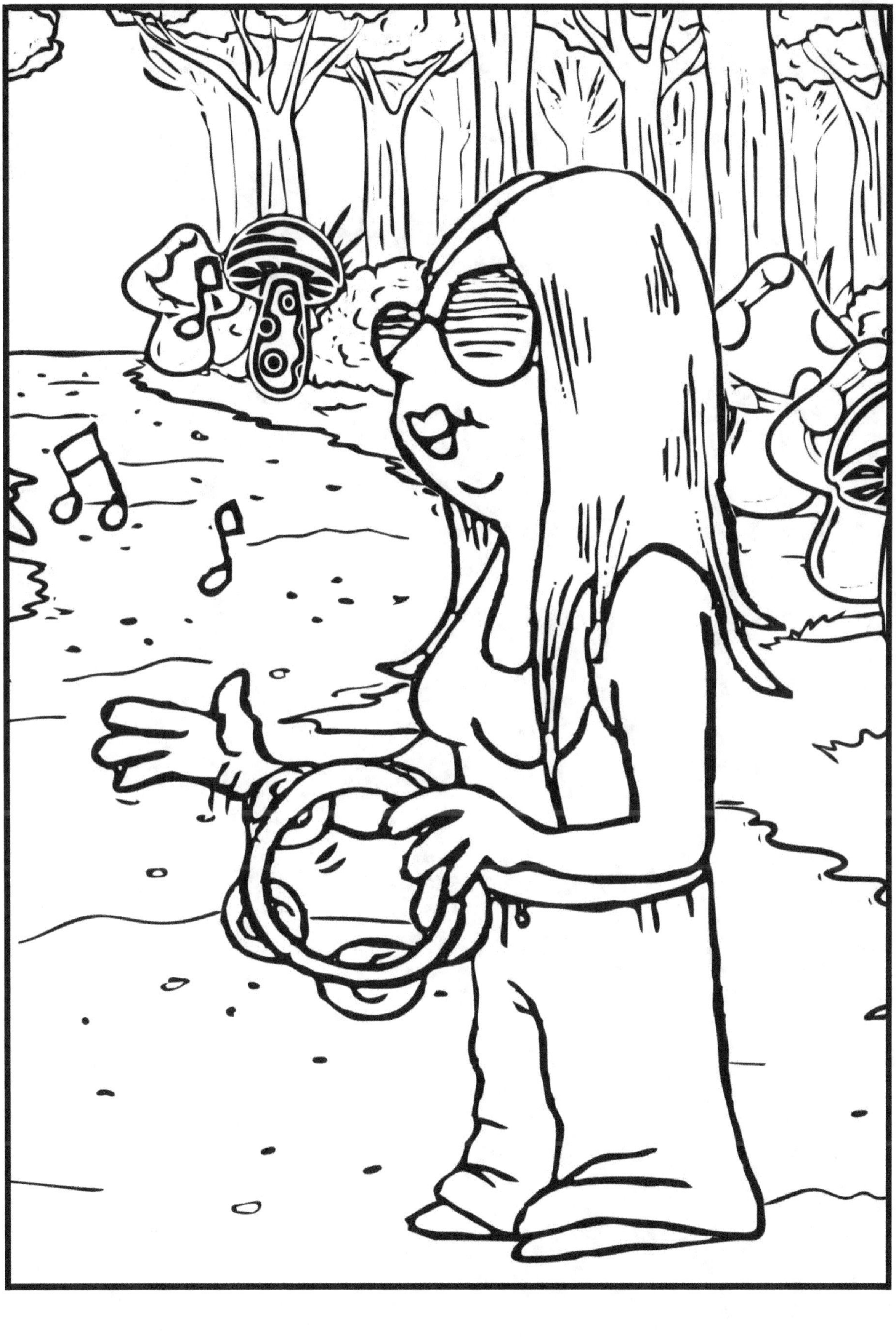

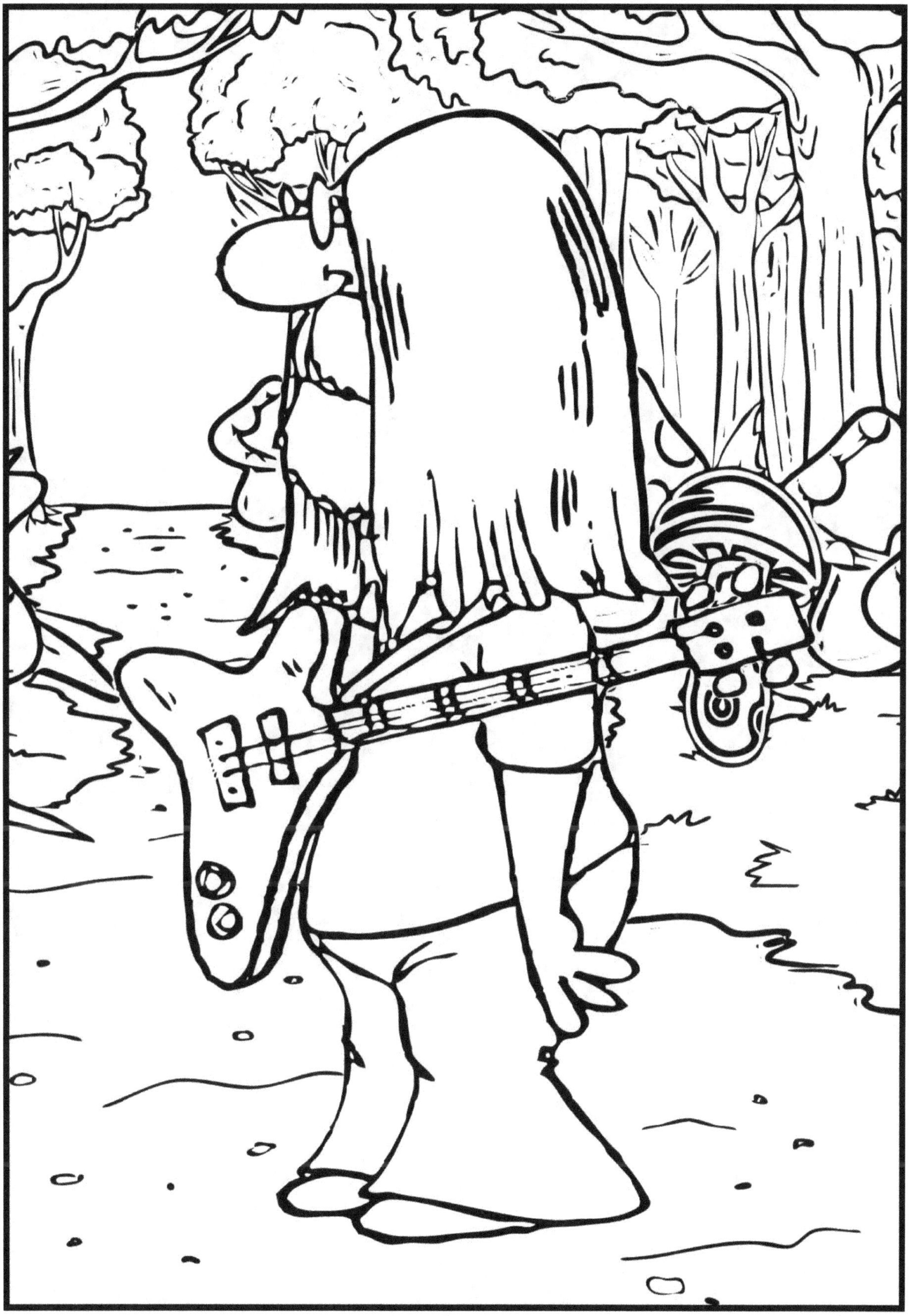

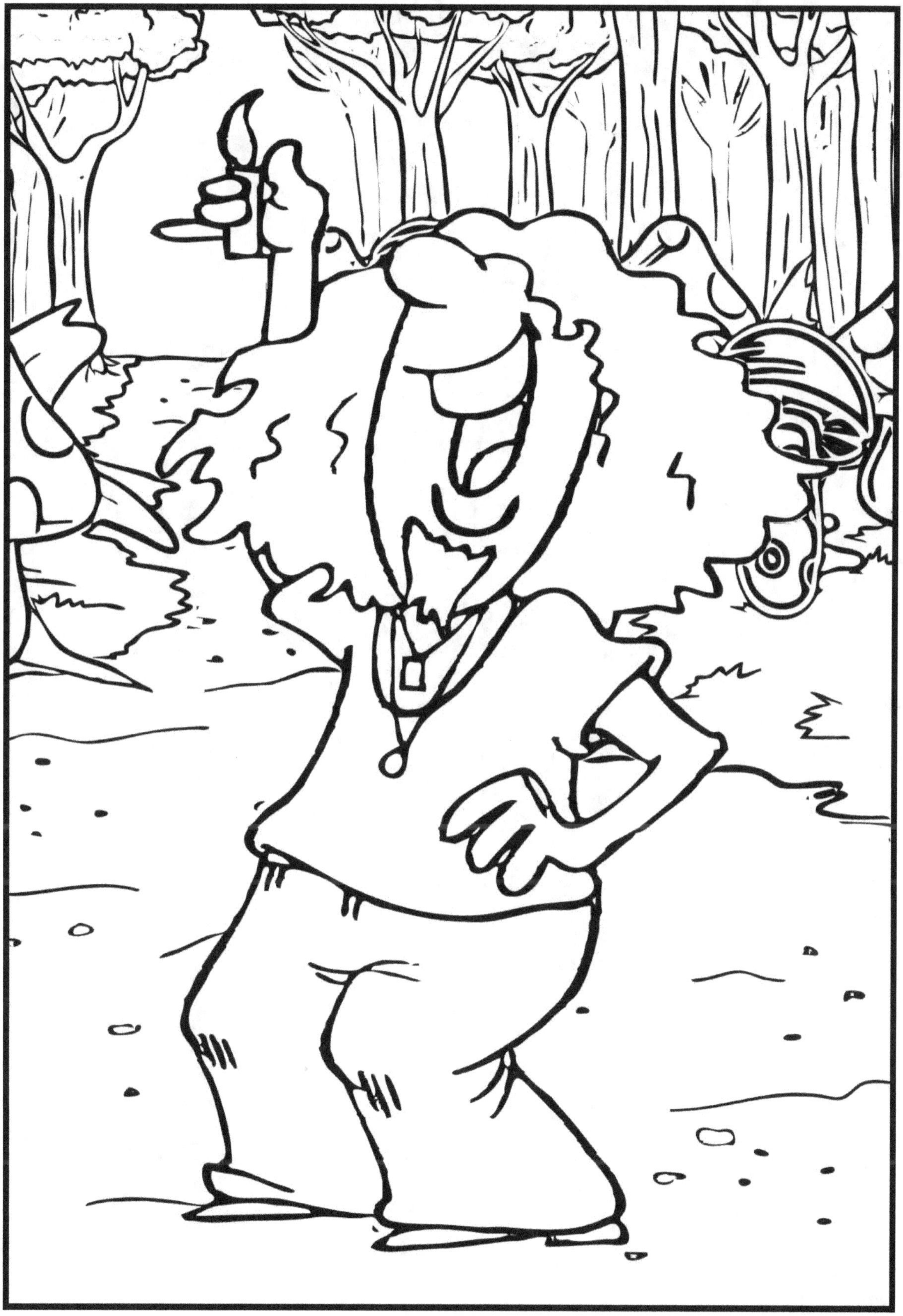

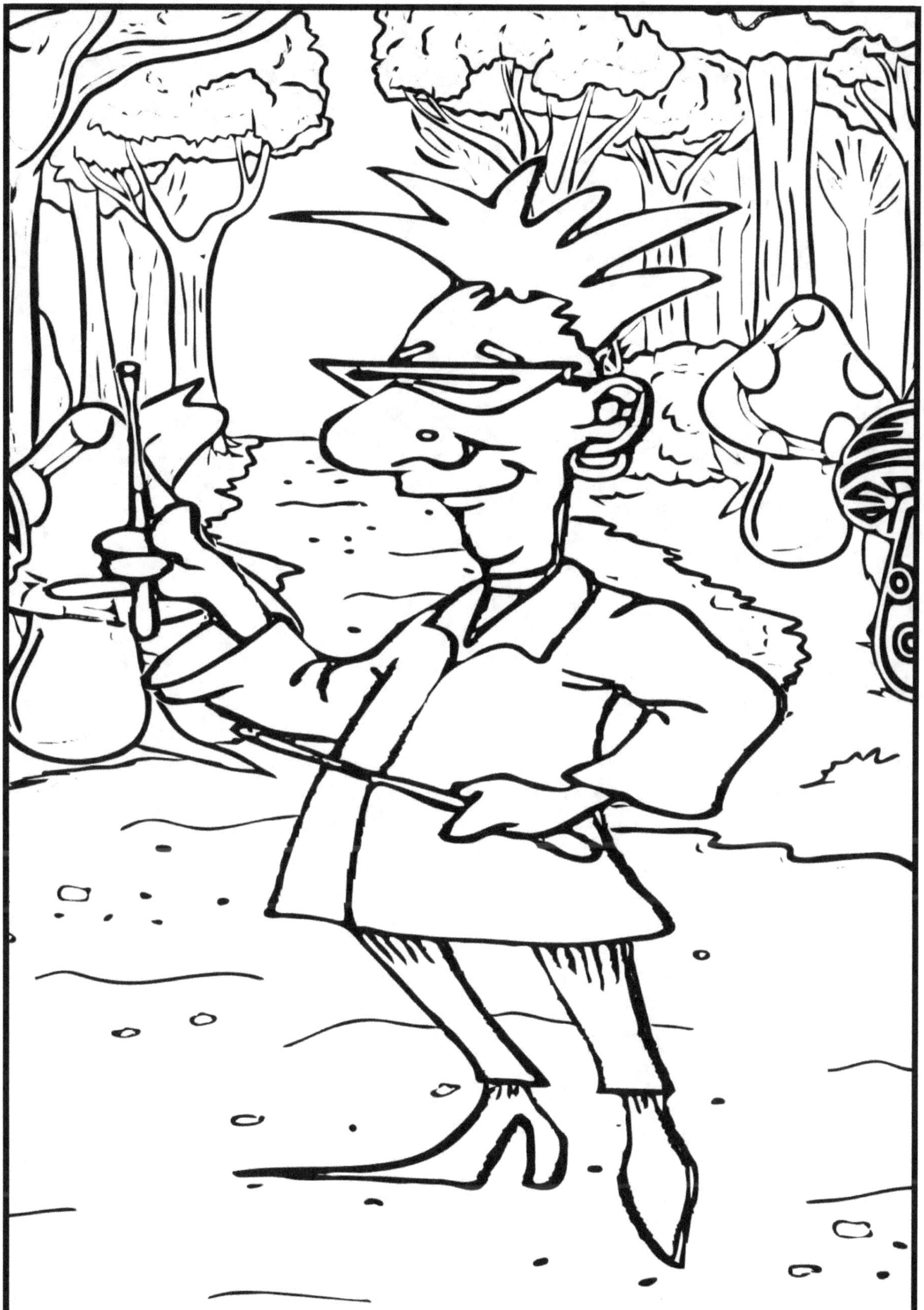

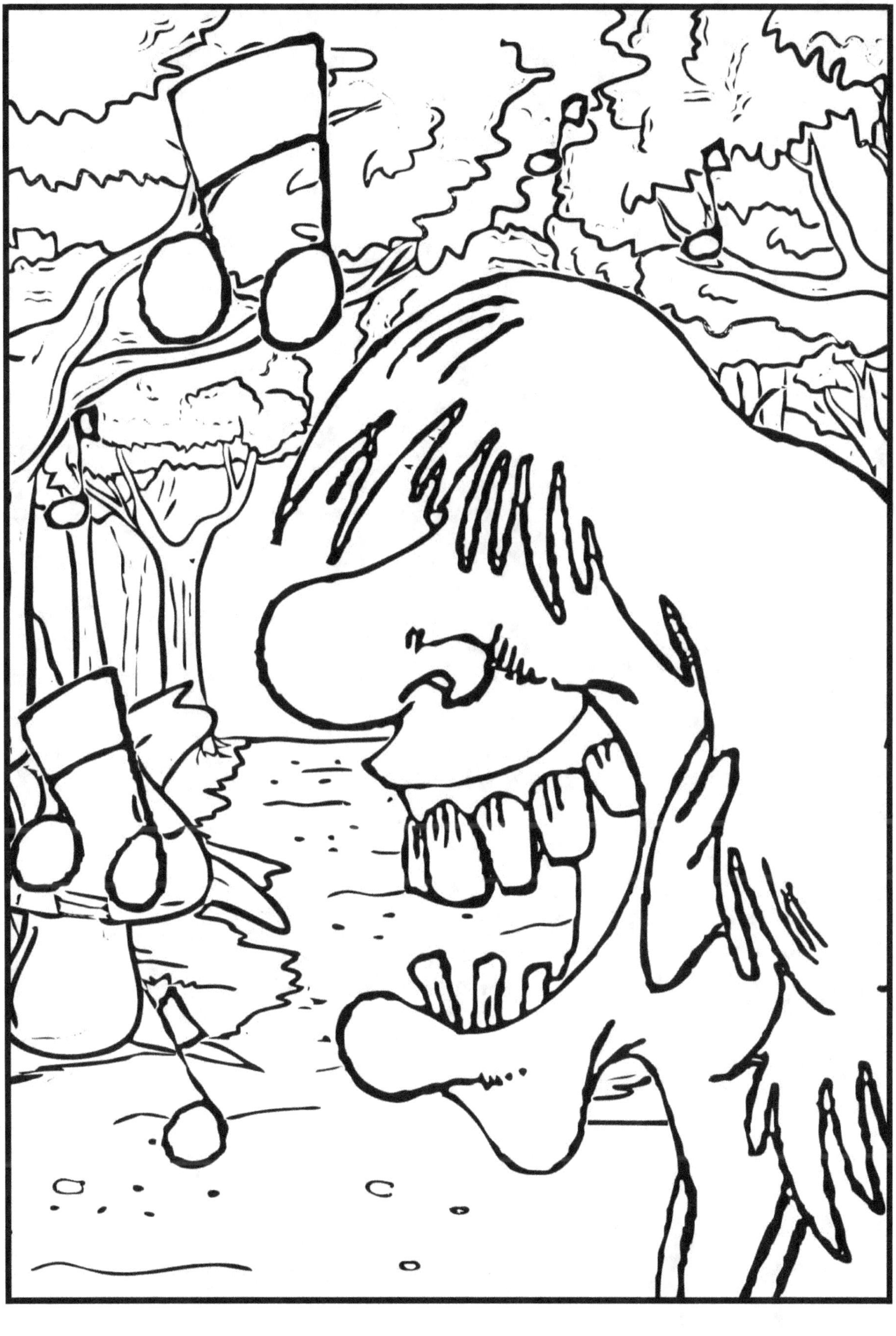

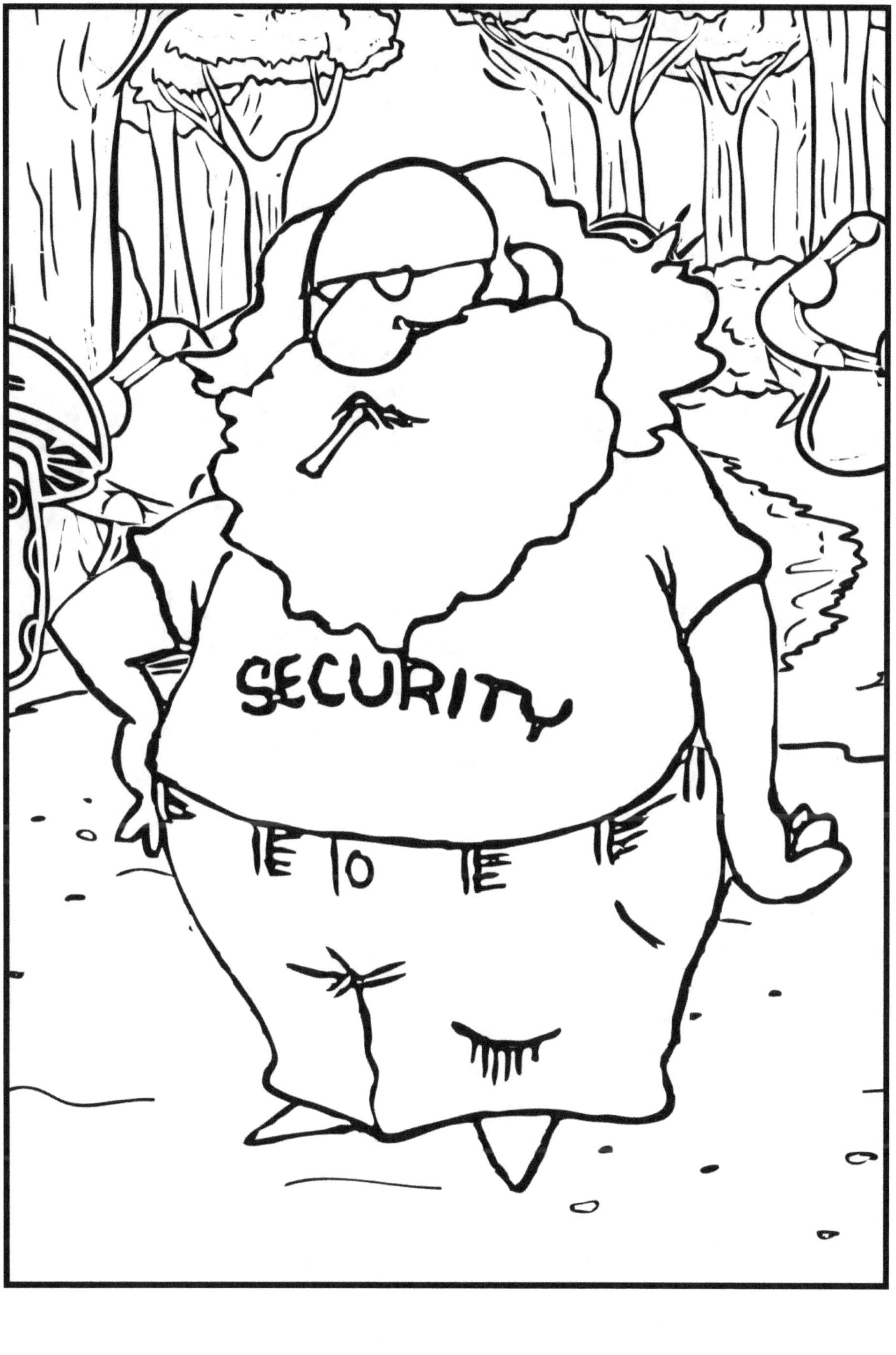
SECURITY

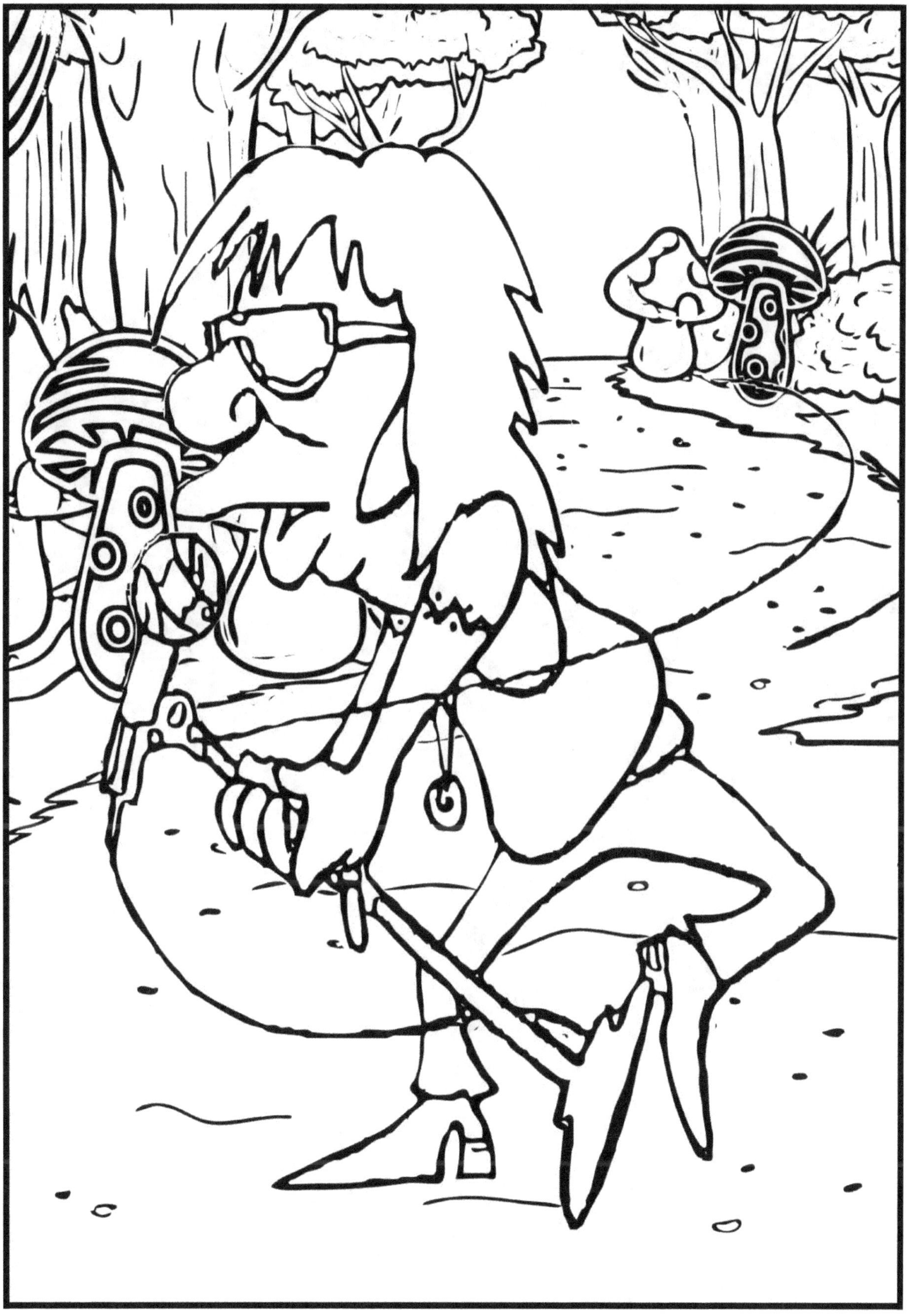

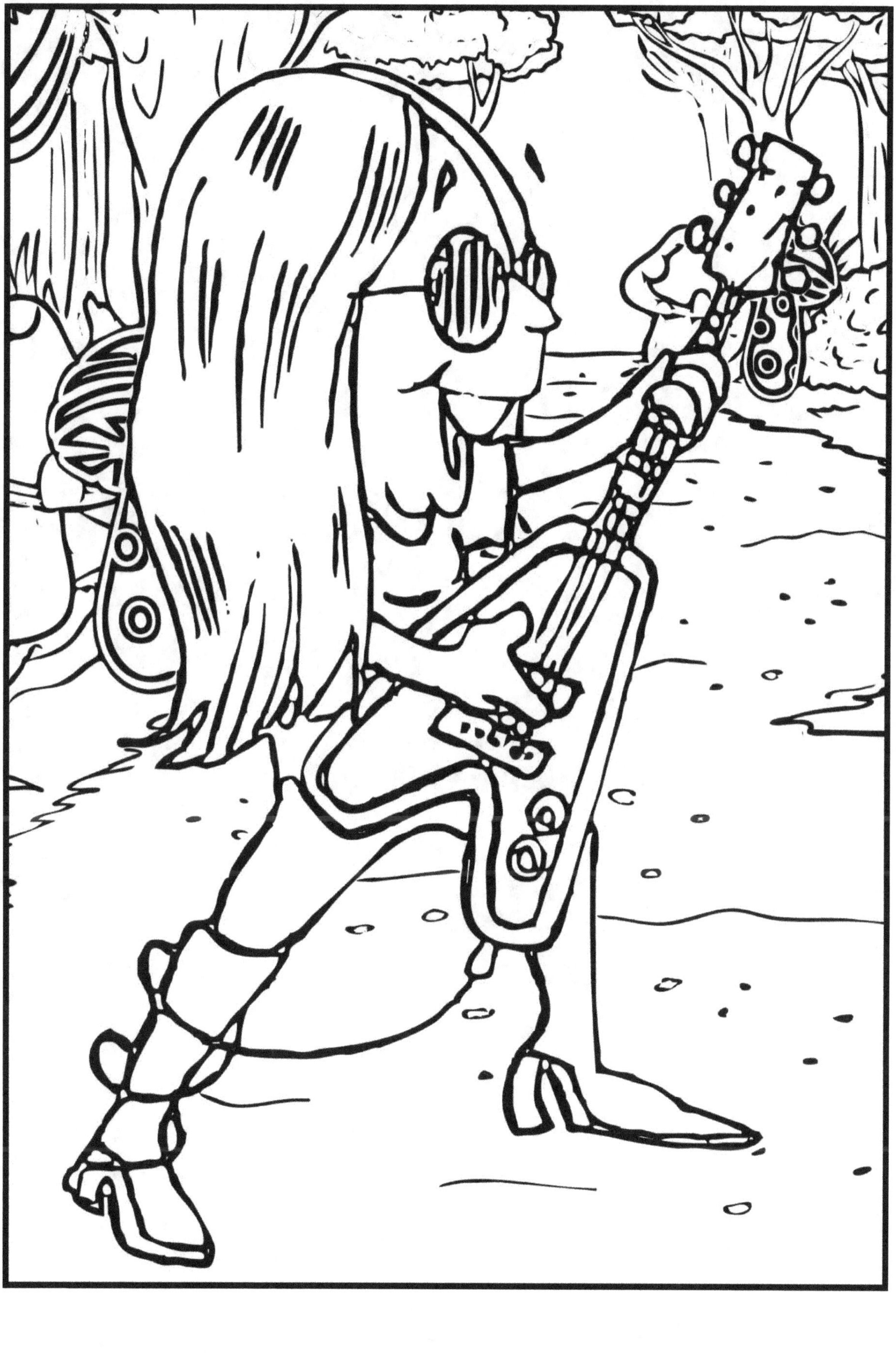

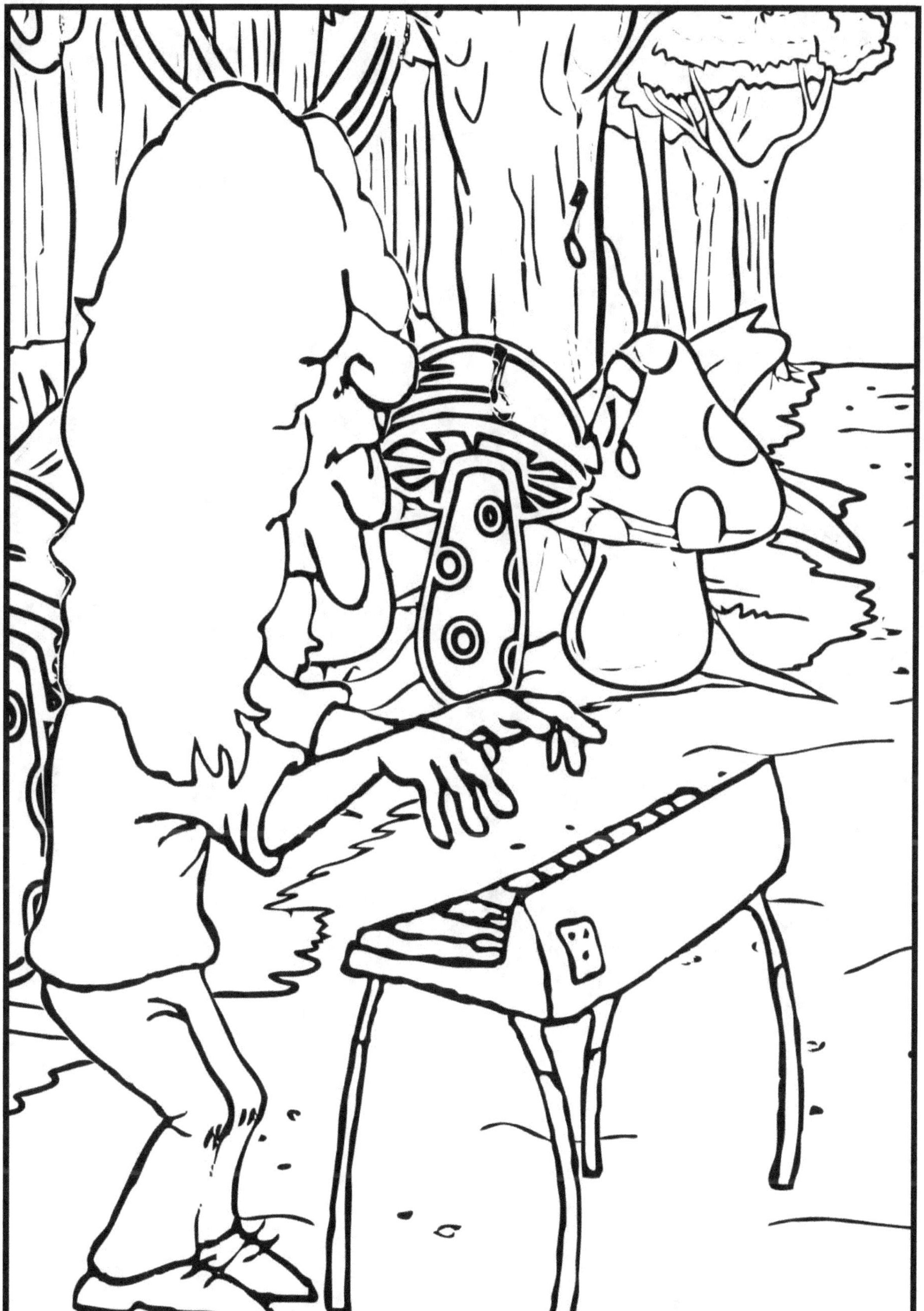

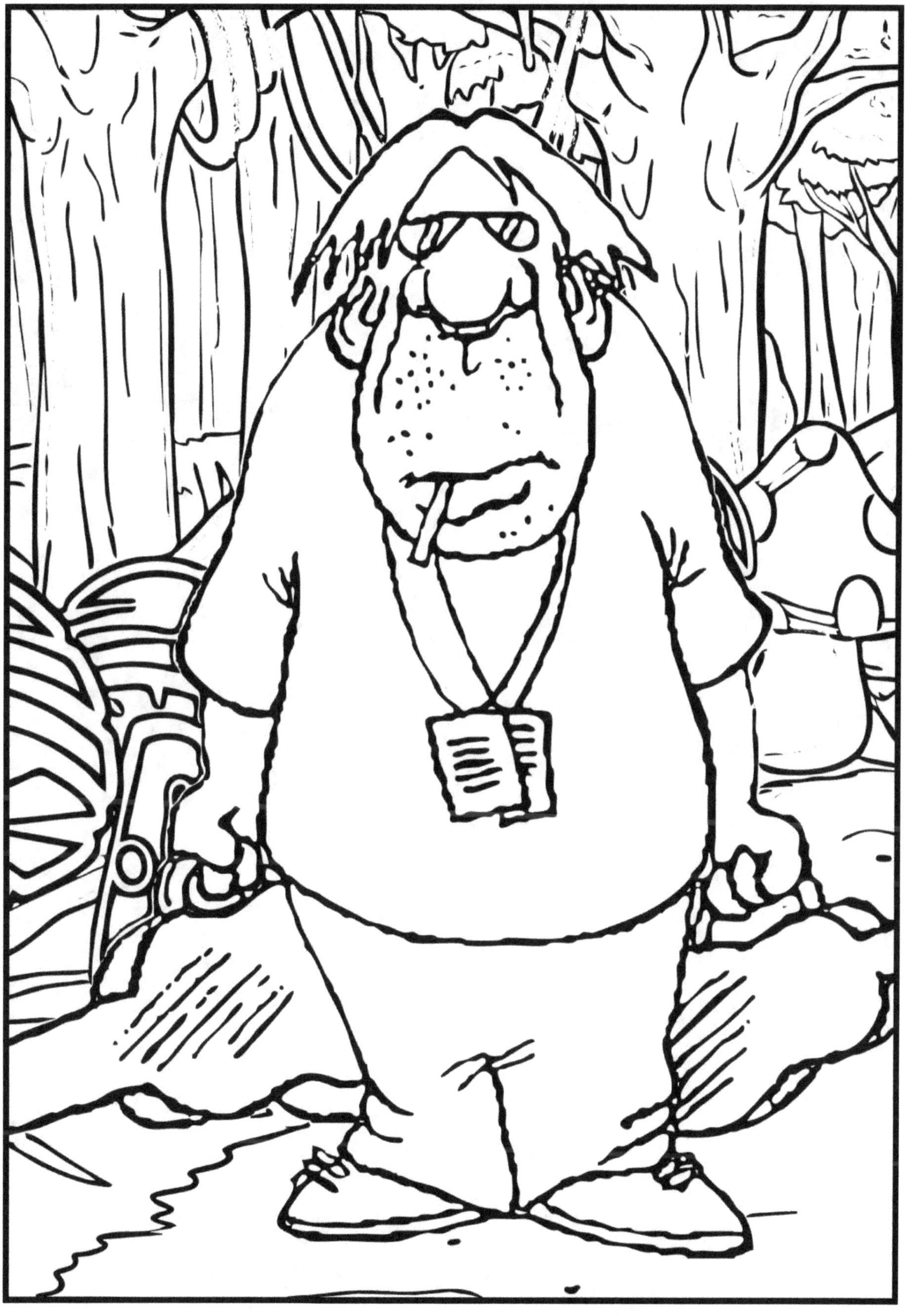

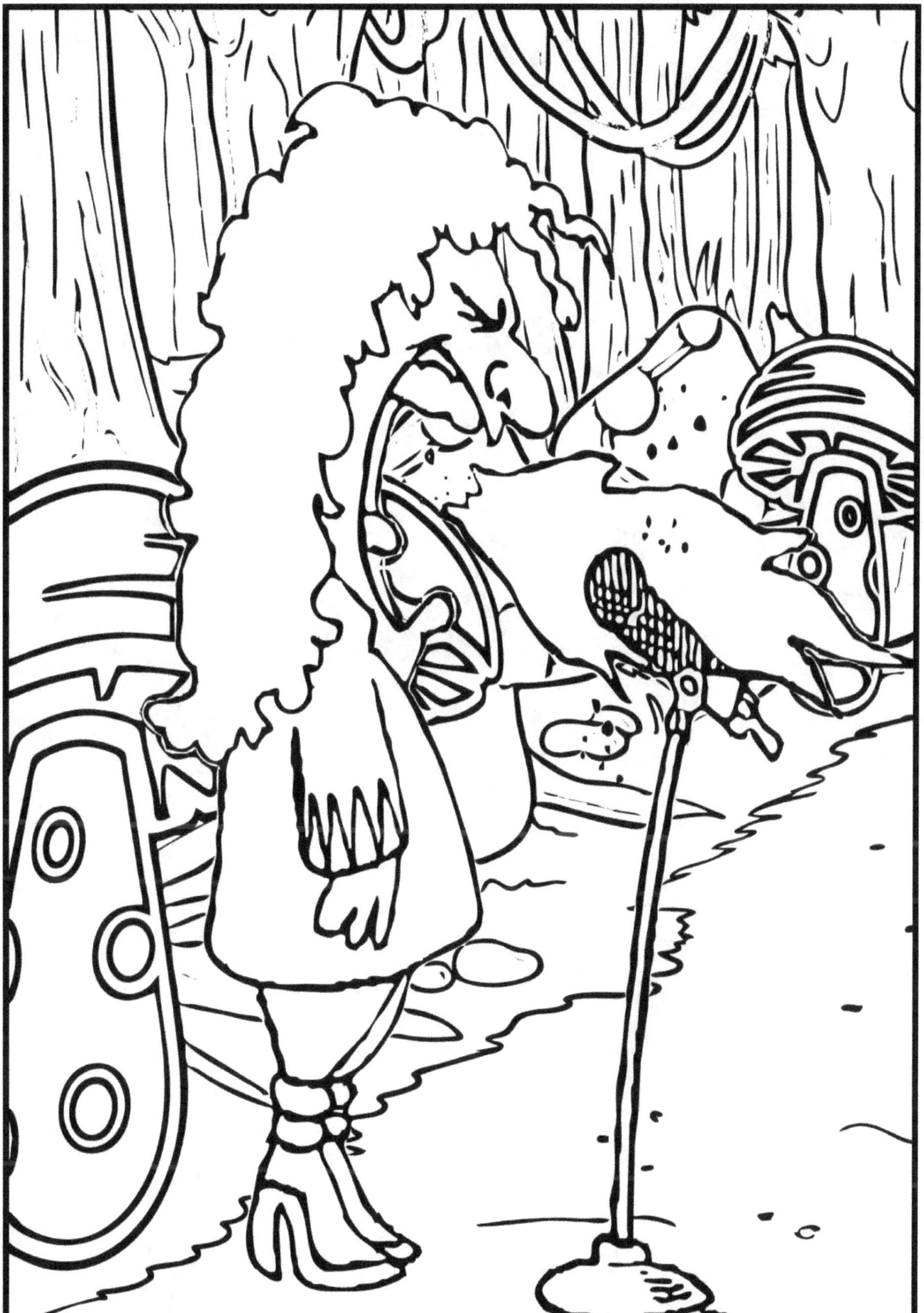

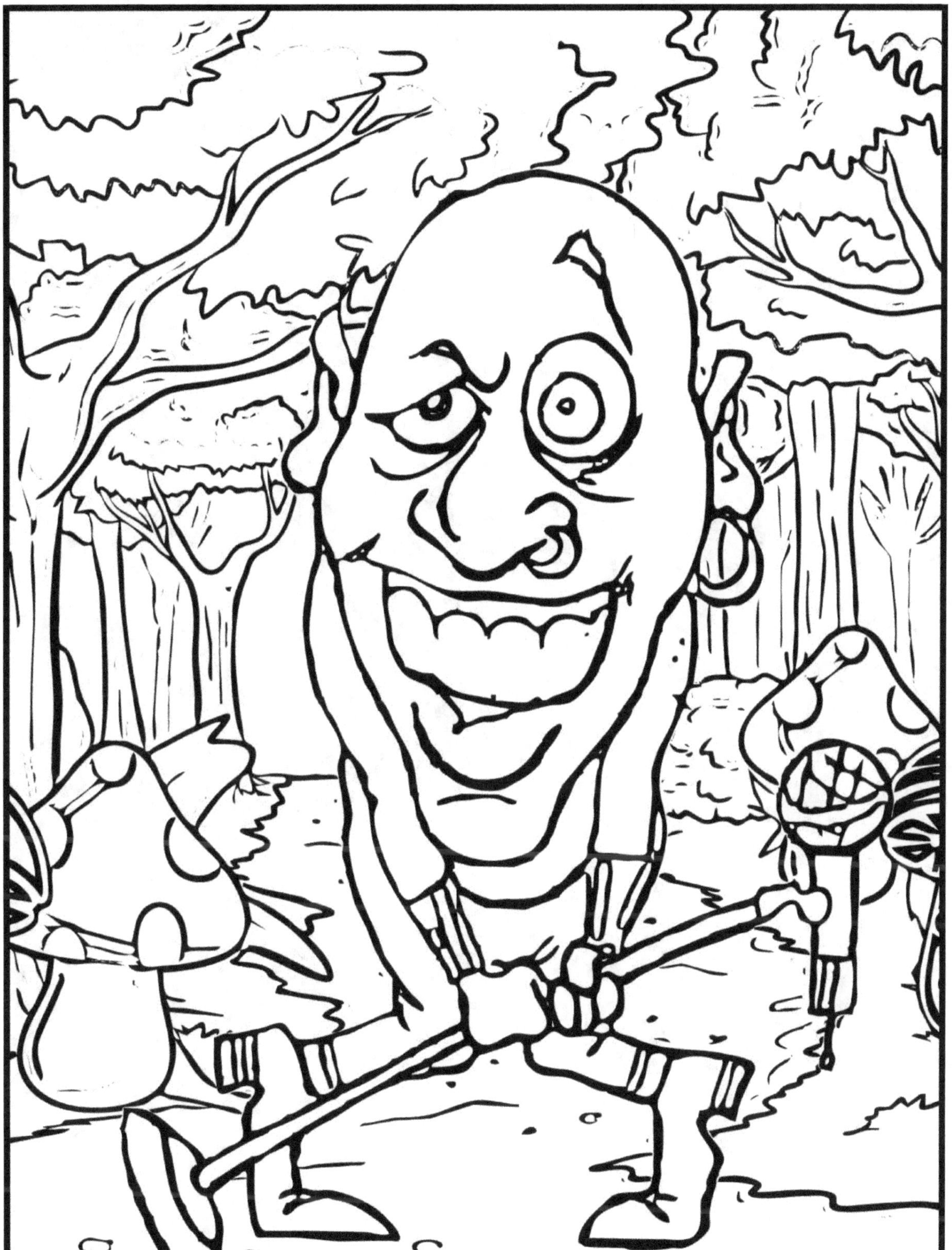

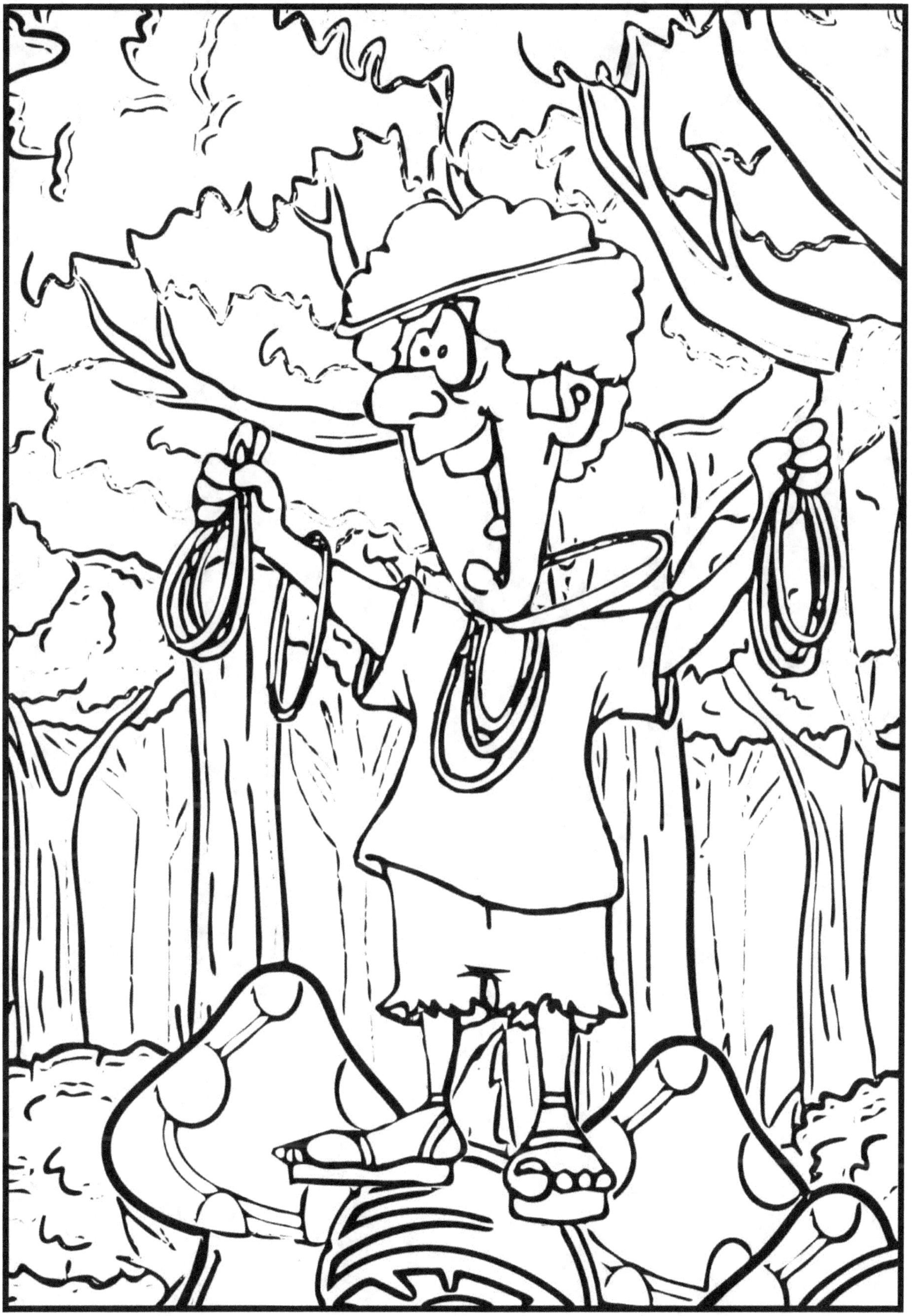

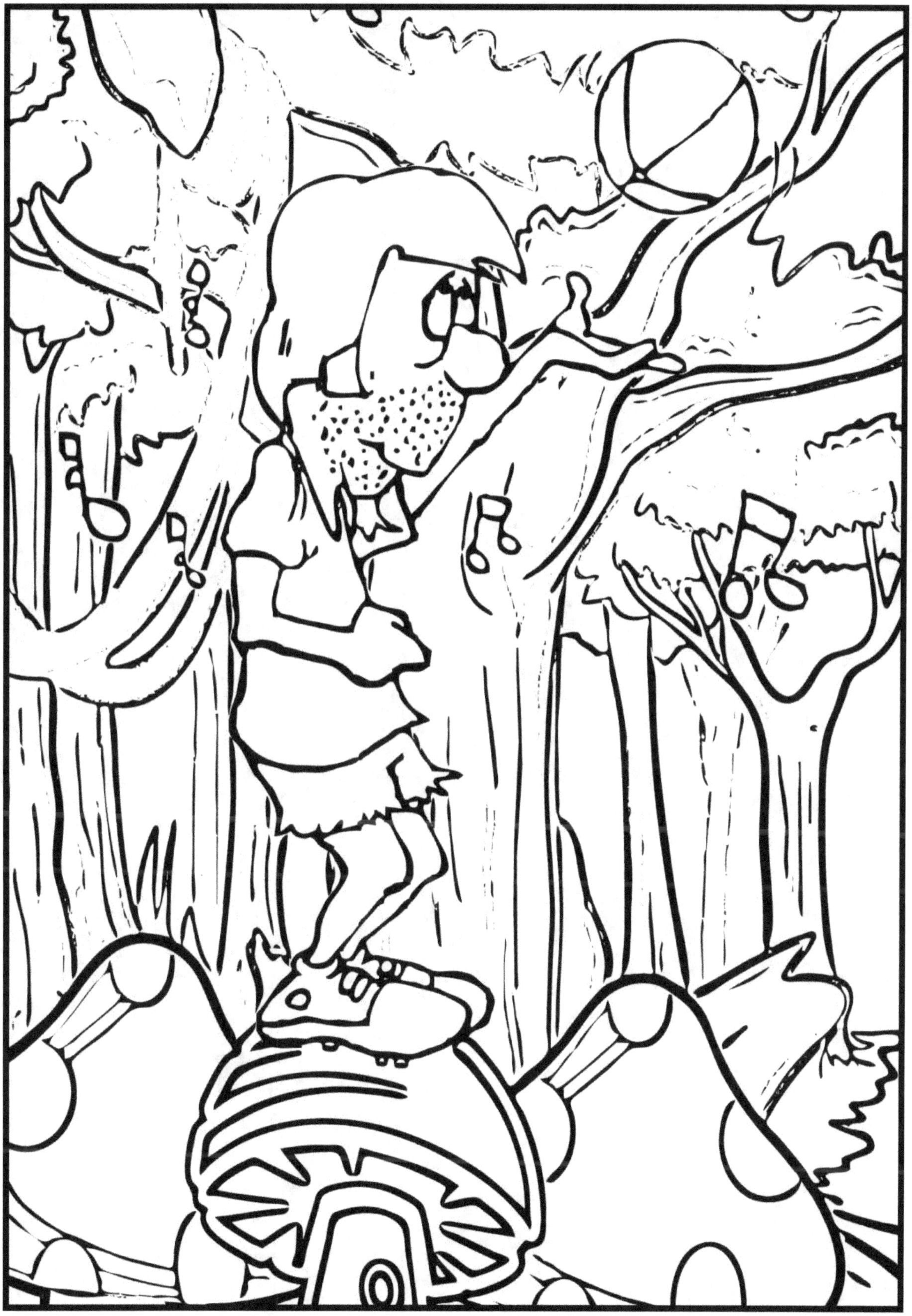

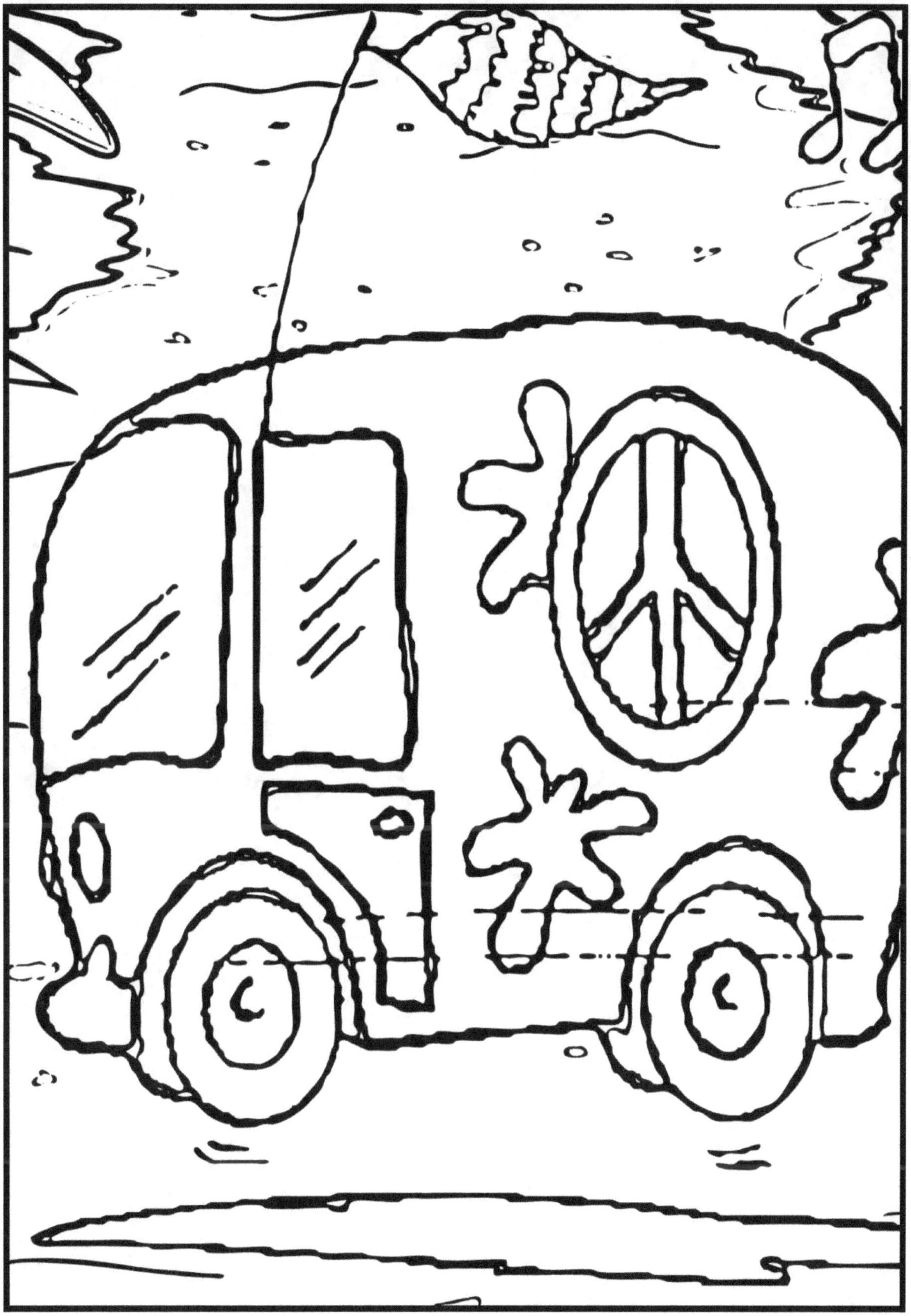

www.ingramcontent.com/pod-product-compliance
Lightning Source LLC
Chambersburg PA
CBHW081559170526
45166CB00009B/2747